Heidegger: A Very Short Introduction

VERY SHORT INTRODUCTIONS are for anyone wanting a stimulating and accessible way in to a new subject. They are written by experts, and have been published in more than 25 languages worldwide.

The series began in 1995, and now represents a wide variety of topics in history, philosophy, religion, science, and the humanities. Over the next few years it will grow to a library of around 200 volumes – a Very Short Introduction to everything from ancient Egypt and Indian philosophy to conceptual art and cosmology.

Very Short Introductions available now:

Available soon:

For more information visit our web site

www.oup.co.uk/vsi

Michael Inwood

HEIDEGGER

A Very Short Introduction

OXFORD
UNIVERSITY PRESS

OXFORD
UNIVERSITY PRESS

Great Clarendon Street, Oxford OX2 6DP

Oxford University Press is a department of the University of Oxford.
It furthers the University's objective of excellence in research, scholarship,
and education by publishing worldwide in

Oxford New York

Auckland Bangkok Buenos Aires Cape Town Chennai
Dar es Salaam Delhi Hong Kong Istanbul Karachi Kolkata
Kuala Lumpur Madrid Melbourne Mexico City Mumbai Nairobi
São Paulo Shanghai Taipei Tokyo Toronto

Oxford is a registered trade mark of Oxford University Press
in the UK and in certain other countries

Published in the United States
by Oxford University Press Inc., New York

British Library Cataloguing in Publication Data

Data available

Library of Congress Cataloging in Publication Data

Data available

ISBN 978-0-19-285410-0

15 17 19 20 18 16 14

Typeset by RefineCatch Ltd, Bungay, Suffolk
Printed in Great Britain by
Ashford Colour Press Ltd, Gosport, Hampshire

Contents

List of Illustrations

References

All references to *Being and Time* are to the pages of the German editions of *Sein und Zeit*. This pagination is indicated in the margins of the English translation, *Being and Time*, tr. J. Macquarrie and E. Robinson (Oxford, 1962). The title of the work is abbreviated as 'BT'. Volumes of the complete edition of Heidegger's works, the *Gesamtausgabe*, published by Vittorio Klostermann of Frankfurt am Main from 1975 on, are referred to by the volume number in lower-case roman numerals, followed by the page reference. (The German pagination is again indicated in the translations.) The volumes referred to, with the dates of *(a)* the original delivery of the lectures, *(b)* the publication of the *Gesamtausgabe* edition, are:

iv   *Erläuterungen zu Hölderlins Dichtung* (*Elucidations to Hölderlin's Poetry*): *(a)* 1936–68; *(b)* 1981, but published first in 1944 and, with additions, in 1971

xvii   *Einführung in die phänomenologische Forschung* (*Introduction to Phenomenological Research*) *(a)* 1923–4; *(b)* 1994

xx   *Prolegomena zur Geschichte des Zeitbegriffs* (*History of the Concept of Time: Prolegomena*, tr. T. Kisiel (Bloomington, Ind., 1985)) *(a)* 1925; *(b)* 1979

xxi   *Logik. Die Frage nach der Wahrheit* (*Logic: The Question about Truth*) *(a)* 1925–6; *(b)* 1976

xxii   *Grundbegriffe der Antiken Philosophie* (*Basic Concepts of Ancient Philosophy*) *(a)* 1926; *(b)* 1993

Other works, all by Heidegger unless otherwise specified, are referred to
by the following abbreviations:

	Phenomenology, tr. D. Cairns (The Hague, 1973) (written in 1929)
CT	*The Concept of Time,* tr. W. McNeill (Oxford, 1992) (lecture given in 1924)
ER	*The Essence of Reasons,* tr. T. Malick (Evanston, 1969) (1st pub. 1929)
HEP	'Hölderlin and the Essence of Poetry', tr. D. Scott, in *Existence and Being,* ed. W. Brock (Chicago, 1949) (lecture given in Rome in 1936)
IM	*An Introduction to Metaphysics,* tr. R. Manheim (New Haven, 1959) (1st pub. 1953, but based on lectures from 1935)
Löwith	*Karl Löwith, My Life in Germany Before and After 1933: A Report,* tr. E. King (London, 1994)
MWP	'My Way to Phenomenology', in *On Time and Being,* tr. J. Stambaugh (New York, 1972), 74–82. (MWP 1st pub. 1963)
N i	*Nietzsche, i. The Will to Power as Art,* tr. D. E. Krell (New York, 1979) (1st pub. 1961, but based on lectures from 1936–7)
OWA	'The Origin of the Work of Art', in Martin Heidegger, *Poetry, Language, Thought,* tr. A. Hofstadter (New York, 1975), 17–87 (OWA 1st pub. 1950 in Heidegger's *Holzwege* (*Woodpaths*))
PR	*The Principle of Reason,* tr. R. Lilly (Bloomington, Ind., 1991) (lectures given in 1956, 1st pub. 1957)
Wolin	*The Heidegger Controversy: A Critical Reader,* ed. R. Wolin (Cambridge, Mass., 1993)

I have sometimes altered the translations given in the above works.

Chapter 1
Heidegger's Life

He was (with the possible exception of Wittgenstein) the greatest philosopher of the twentieth century. He was (with the possible exception of Hegel) the greatest charlatan ever to claim the title of 'philosopher', a master of hollow verbiage masquerading as profundity. He was an irredeemable German redneck, and, for a time, a gullible and self-important Nazi. He was a pungent, if inevitably covert, critic of Nazism, a discerning analyst of the ills of our age and our best hope of a cure for them. Each of these claims has been advanced, with greater or lesser plausibility, on Heidegger's behalf. Who was the man who provokes these contrasting reactions?

Martin Heidegger was born on 26 September 1889, to a poor Catholic family in the small town of Messkirch in Baden in south-west Germany. His father Friedrich was the cellarman and sexton of the local church. In 1903 Martin went to the high school at Konstanz, where he was supported by a scholarship and lived in a Catholic boarding-house. He was, by this time, being prepared for the priesthood. In 1906 he moved to the high school in Freiburg where the church supplied him with free board and lodging. It was here, by his own account, that his interest in philosophy was first aroused, by a work *On the Various Meanings of Being according to Aristotle* (1862), by Franz Brentano, one of the forebears of the phenomenological movement. Later he came across Carl Braig's *On Being: An Outline of Ontology* (1896), which contained excerpts from Aristotle and from medieval philosophers such as Aquinas (MWP, 74). In 1909 he left the high school and became a Jesuit novice, but was discharged within a month owing to heart trouble and perhaps also his lack of a spiritual vocation. He then entered Freiburg University, and studied theology and scholastic philosophy. In 1911 he underwent a crisis that led him to break off his training for the priesthood and turn to the study of philosophy and the moral and natural sciences. It was at this time that he studied modern philosophy, especially the *Logical Investigations* of Edmund Husserl, the leading figure in the phenomenological movement, whose aim was systematic enquiry into our conscious mental processes without regard to their non-mental causes and consequences. He graduated in 1913 with a dissertation on *The Theory of the Judgement in Psychologism*, in which he criticized, in the spirit of Husserl, attempts to analyse the logical notion of a judgement in terms of human psychology. In 1915 his habilitation thesis on *Duns Scotus's Theory of Categories and Meaning* earned him the right to lecture at the University.

Heidegger's academic career was interrupted by the First World War. In 1915 he was conscripted, but was regarded as unsuitable for combat duties and assigned to the postal and meteorological services. In 1917 he married a Protestant, Elfriede Petri, and, shortly after the birth of their son Jorg; in January 1919, he announced his breach with the 'system of Catholicism'. On his discharge from the army in 1918 he had become an unsalaried lecturer at Freiburg and an assistant to Husserl, who had become professor at the University in 1916. Heidegger now began to win fame as a teacher of dazzling brilliance and insight. His lectures on Aristotle, on St Paul, on St Augustine, on phenomenology, on the world of our everyday experience and the human being, earned him acclaim as the 'hidden king' of philosophy (Arendt). In 1923 he moved to Marburg as associate professor and there he became friends with the theologian Rudolf Bultmann and began an enduring relationship with Harmah Arendt. (His friendship and correspondence with Karl Jaspers had begun in 1920.) At Marburg he extended the

1. The town hall and market square of Messkirch

range of his lectures with courses on Aristotle's *Rhetoric*, Plato's *Sophist*, presocratic Greek philosophy, time, truth, Aquinas, Kant, and Leibniz. He had not, however, published for ten years. And then in the spring of 1927 he published his great work, *Being and Time*, in the *Yearbook for Philosophy and Phenomenological Research*, edited by Husserl, and also as a separate volume. His reason for publishing it at this time was, he tells us, to meet government requirements for appointment to a full professorship at Marburg (MWP, 80). In the following year he succeeded Husserl to the chair at Freiburg. His inaugural lecture, in 1929, was entitled 'What is Metaphysics?' – a subject on which he lectured at greater length in the following winter (though, in his characteristic manner, much of his course on 'The Fundamental Concepts of Metaphysics' is devoted to the apparently extraneous topics of boredom and insects). In that year too he engaged in a public debate with Ernst Cassirer on Kant's philosophy and published *Kant and the Problem of Metaphysics*. He lectured too on the German idealists Schelling and Hegel, on the allegory of the cave in Plato's *Republic*, and on the presocratic philosophers Anaximander and Parmenides. In 1930 he rejected an offer of a chair in Berlin. Heidegger was deeply attached to the provincial life of southern Germany, to its small towns and rugged landscape – he did much of his writing in a mountain cottage at Todtnauberg, which he had built in 1923. He disliked big cities and their social and cultural life.

The period of the Weimar Republic, from 1918 to 1933, was marked by intense cultural activity, but also by economic distress and political turmoil. In September 1930 Adolf Hitler's National Socialist German Workers' Party (NSDAP, but commonly known as 'Nazi') became the second largest party in Germany. On 30 January 1933 Hitler was appointed chancellor in a right-wing coalition. The Reichstag fire on 27 February gave him an excuse for rushing through decrees conferring absolute power on the Nazi party. On 30 June 1934, on the pretext of Ernst Röhm's rebellion, he murdered his rivals Röhm's Storm Troopers and other inconvenient party members, such as Gregor Strasser, a 'left-wing' Nazi more opposed to capitalism than to Jews or Bolshevism. (Josef Goebbels had earlier been a supporter of Strasser, but was converted by Hitler in 1926 to a programme that could win the backing of bankers and industrialists.) On 2 August 1934 Hitler was proclaimed 'Führer of the German Reich' ('Leader of the German Empire'). In the 1920s Heidegger had been virtually apolitical, but by the early 1930s he had become sympathetic to Nazism. On 21 April 1933 he was elected rector of Freiburg University by the faculty, and on 1 May he joined the NSDAP. On 27 May he gave his rectoral address, 'The Self-Affirmation of the German University', which, though not an especially reassuring document, is noticeably free of anti-Semitism. (He did, however, place labour, military service, and knowledge on an equal footing as duties of the student.) During his period as rector Heidegger co-operated with the new regime, while trying to moderate some of its cruder aspects. He campaigned for Germany's withdrawal from the League of Nations in the plebiscite of November 1933. Conflicts with the faculty and with party officials led him to resign as rector in April 1934 and, though he did not leave the party, he took no further significant part in political affairs. He later claimed that he became disillusioned with Nazism after the Röhm *putsch*.

Heidegger published little in the 1930s but continued to lecture, especially on art. In 1935 he spoke, in Freiburg, on 'The Origin of the Work of Art'. He went to Rome in 1936 to give the first of many lectures on Hölderlin, the cryptic philosophical poet who had been Hegel's room-mate at the Tubingen theological college in the late eighteenth century. In Rome he met Karl Lowith, a former pupil of Jewish descent, who claimed that Heidegger retained his allegiance to Nazism (Lowith, 59–61). In the same year he began his lectures on Nietzsche, which continued into the early 1940s and were published in 1961. Heidegger's friends claim that these lectures contained covert criticism of Nazism and tried to rescue Nietzsche from the use made of him to support racist doctrines and practices. Heidegger was at this time under surveillance by the Gestapo. From 1938 on technology assumed a larger role in his thought. This interest appeared in a Freiburg lecture of 1938, 'The Establishment of the Modern World-Picture by Metaphysics' and also in a seminar on Ernst Jünger's essay 'The Worker'. (Jünger was neither a Nazi nor anti-Semitic, but some of his ideas, such as 'total mobilization', were adopted by the Nazis.) Heidegger's lectures in this period often refer to political events and later to the War. He always relates them to the 'forgetfulness of Being' and to technology. The wilful construction of a world-empire to last for millennia shows, he argued, a preference for quantity over quality that is alien to genuine creators like the Greeks. Empire-building stems not primarily from 'dictators' and 'authoritarian states', but from the 'metaphysical essence of modernity', the will to mastery over nature (li. 17f.). This verdict on Nazism was delivered in the summer of 1941, when Hitler's power was at its height.

In the autumn of 1944 Heidegger was (humiliatingly) drafted into the Volkssturm (the 'People's Storm', something like the British Home Guard or 'Dad's Army') to help dig anti-tank ditches along the Rhine. At the beginning of 1945 he went to Messkirch to arrange his manuscripts and secure their safety. In June, two months after Germany's final collapse, he went to Freiburg and appeared before the 'Denazification Commission'. Some officers of the French occupying forces made contact with him, and arrangements were made for him to meet his long-time admirer Jean-Paul Sartre. This plan miscarried, but he corresponded with Sartre and struck up a friendship with Jean Beaufret, the most loyal of French Heideggerians. In 1946 he was forbidden to teach; the ban lasted until 1949. He was, however, permitted to keep his library and was granted an emeritus professorship by the University. This verdict was supported by the University authorities, as well as by the French administration. It was based in part on a report by his old friend Jaspers.

Heidegger's career as a writer and lecturer soon revived. He presented 'What are Poets for?' (1946) to a small audience in memory of Rilke's death twenty years earlier. He published *On Humanism* (1947), a letter to Beaufret in which he distanced his own philosophy from French existentialism. In December 1949 he gave four lectures to the Bremen Club, and one of these, 'The Thing', was delivered at the Bavarian Academy of Fine Arts in 1950. He renewed old friendships: Arendt visited him in 1950, and his correspondence with her, and also with Jaspers, revived. He lectured again to the Bavarian Academy in 1953, this time on 'The Question of Technology'. He travelled more widely than hitherto. He lectured on 'What is Philosophy?' at Cérisy-la-Salle in 1955, and later on 'Hegel and the Greeks' (1957) at Aix-en-Provence, where he also became friends with René Char. On his seventieth birthday in 1959 he was made an honorary citizen of Messkirch. He visited Greece for the first time in 1962, and again in 1967, when he addressed the Academy of Sciences and Arts in Athens on 'The Source of Art and the Vocation of Thinking'. From 1966 to 1973 he gave a series of seminars, in Le Thor in Provence and later in Zaehringen. He attempted to justify his conduct during the Nazi era in an interview with *Der Spiegel* in 1966. This was published after his death ten years later, and bears the title 'Only a god can save us', a remark he made in the interview which recalls a poem of Hölderlin: 'In my boyhood days / Often a god would save me / From the shouts and the rod of men'.

After the War Heidegger had steadily published works that were, for the most part, revised versions of his lectures. In his last days he helped to prepare a complete edition of his works, which was to include transcripts of his lectures as well as works published earlier. He declared his wish that no thought he had expressed in a lecture would be lost. A volume of this edition appeared in 1975, containing the Marburg lectures on 'The Basic Problems of Phenomenology' from the summer of 1927. (The edition is not yet complete; it is projected to fill about a hundred volumes.) Heidegger died in 1976 on 26 May, and was buried on 28 May in the churchyard at Messkirch next to his parents. A Catholic mass was held in his memory. The officiating priest, his nephew Heinrich Heidegger, quoted Jeremiah 1: 7: 'But the Lord said unto me, Say not, I am a child: for thou shalt go to all that I shall send thee, and whatsoever I command thee thou shalt speak.'

Heidegger's life is an intriguing tale of a wanderer's return, but what makes it more interesting than many other such lives is his status as a thinker. No one would fret over the details of his political activity, let alone his religious beliefs or private life, were he not a significant philosopher. To his philosophy, then, we now turn.

Chapter 2
Heidegger's Philosophy

Heidegger's admirers differ over whether he produced a *second* great work, and if so, which it is; the Nietzsche lectures or the *Contributions to Philosophy (Of the Event)*, drafted between 1936 and 1938, but published only in 1989, as well as other works, are often nominated. But there is general agreement that he wrote one great work, and that it is *Being and Time*.

Being and Time bears comparison with Hegel's *Phenomenology of Spirit*, if not with Plato's *Republic* or Kant's *Critique of Pure Reason*. It is by far the most influential of his writings: it has made its mark on theologians, psychologists, and sociologists as well as philosophers. It crystallizes the results of his reading, lecturing, and thinking over the previous decade, and it points the way ahead to his later works, which even if they differ considerably from *Being and Time* cannot be understood independently of it. It is at the same time one of the most difficult books ever written. Both its overall structure and the language in which it is composed present great problems to the reader, especially to the non-German reader.

The argument of the work, in rough outline, is this: It is important to ask the question 'What is Being?', a question which was once asked but has long been forgotten. To do this we need to consider some being or entity, and the obvious choice is the human being or 'Dasein',

2. Heidegger as a schoolboy, in about 1899

since that is the being that asks the question and which has a preconceptual understanding of being which, if used with caution, will guide us towards an answer to our question. Hence the first section of the book is devoted to a 'preparatory fundamental analysis of Dasein', which argues that Dasein is essentially 'in the world' and that its being is 'care'. In the second section he introduces a theme which was only implicit in the first, Dasein's temporality. Dasein is essentially temporal: it looks ahead to its own death, it surveys its life as a whole in conscience and resoluteness, it is essentially historical. Dasein's being is intimately bound up with temporality. *Being and Time* was originally intended to have a third section, which was to consider the question of Being as such and its relationship to time, in greater independence of Dasein. This section has never appeared, but the preface to the seventh edition of *Being and Time* (1953) refers us to his *Introduction to Metaphysics* (1953, but based on lectures from 1935), in which he considers the contrasts between being, on the one hand, and, on the other, becoming, appearance, thinking, and ought. (In a marginal note to his copy of BT, he refers to *The Basic Problems of Phenomenology* (1927, 1975), as a substitute for the missing third section. This work is itself incomplete, dealing with little over a half of its promised contents.) BT was also intended to have a second part, itself consisting of three sections, which were to deal respectively with Kant, Descartes, and Aristotle. (Heidegger likes to do the history of philosophy backwards: a philosopher is unmasked to reveal the face of a predecessor on whom he covertly depends, a face which is in turn exposed as a mask . . .) This part too did not appear, but his other works and lectures give a better picture of its intended contents than we have of the missing section of the first part.

Even this brief survey of BT raises questions about it. What is the question of being and why is it so important to ask it? What is Dasein and how is it related to the question of being? How and why is Dasein in the world? Why are time and temporality so crucial to Dasein and its being? What did Heidegger propose to say in the missing sections

11

of BT and how, if at all, is it related to what he says in later works? These and other questions will be considered in the following chapters.

Chapter 3
Being

Why being? The term 'being' enters into a variety of contrasts. It contrasts, in the first place, with 'knowledge' and with 'science'. Many philosophers in Heidegger's day and earlier, especially those who claimed to follow Kant, were concerned mainly with epistemology or the theory of knowledge, asking such questions as 'What can we know?' and 'What are the foundations of the sciences?' Heidegger was averse to epistemology: it 'continually sharpens the knife but never gets round to cutting' (lviii. 4). Knowledge, especially the systematic knowledge of science, involves a relation, knowing, between a knower, on the one hand, and an object, or range of objects, known about, on the other. Heidegger's doubts about epistemology concern each of the three elements.

Take first the knower. What is it? Is it a pure subject wholly absorbed in the disinterested, theoretical knowledge of its subject-matter, or is it an interested human being, situated in a particular place and a particular time, with many other relations and attitudes to many other things than the objects of its science? Take secondly the relation of knowing. Why knowing? Knowing is only one relation among many that we may take up to the things of the world; it is not the first relation we adopt towards them, it is taken up fairly late in one's career, and then only sporadically; nor is it the most obvious attitude to take towards, say, one's spouse or the key to one's own front door.

How is knowing related to these other attitudes to things? And what does knowing consist in? We tend to speak as if knowing were a uniform thing, as if electrons were known in the same way as historical events. Or if we notice that this is not so we are tempted, like Descartes, to propose an ideal form of knowledge which will guarantee unerring results about, say, the dimensions and movements of material particles. But this will not do for, say, historical events, which are thereby excluded from the realm of knowable objects. If we decline this course, then we realize that the right way of getting to know about a range of entities depends in part on the nature or being of those entities. We know about historical events in one way, and about electrons in another: we do not sift ancient documents to find out about electrons or try to detect Napoleon in a laboratory. This is because historical events are a different sort of entity from electrons. So before we deal with knowledge, we need to consider the nature, or the being, of the object known.

Objects or entities fall into classes: numbers, plants, stars, animals, and so on. A class of entities is often the preserve of a special science. The astronomer studies stars, the botanist plants, and so on. If the philosopher is to study being rather than knowledge, should he too study stars and plants, differing from the scientific specialist only in the breadth and generality of his knowledge, with its attendant superficiality? No. This would not only consign the philosopher to a lower status than Heidegger is ready to tolerate, it would miss a prior, more fundamental question about the objects of the sciences. How do we come to divide up the world of entities in this way? The world does not naturally present itself to us carved up in readiness for the sciences. When two lovers walk hand in hand across a meadow under a starry sky, they do not see themselves and their surroundings as objects separated out for the geologist, the botanist, the meteorologist, even if they are themselves, say, geologists in their professional lives. Once there were no such refined boundaries between sciences and their object-ranges as there now are. Even in recent times scientists sometimes redefine the nature of their subject-matter: they redraw the boundary around it, form a new conception of what lies within it, open up new ways of knowing about their objects and close off old ones. What is such a scientist doing but projecting a view of being onto entities, a projection of a sort which ultimately underlies the work of any science?

This, however, raises another problem. If the scientist, at least the reflective, innovative scientist, considers the being of his subject-matter, what is there left for the philosopher to do? Why not leave it to the scientist? Because, Heidegger argues, the scientist is concerned only with one among several 'regions' of beings; as a scientist he ignores the background against which his projection takes place, the objects left for other sciences and the familiar articles of use that we rely on every day, but which elude the theoretical sciences altogether. Not to mention the nature of being as such or the informal overall understanding of being that enables him to highlight one area of being in particular.

The Various Meanings of Being

Heidegger may have convinced us that we should focus on entities rather than on our knowledge of entities or on the sciences. But 'being' for Heidegger contrasts not only with knowledge, but also with 'beings' or 'entities'. Why being rather than beings? We know of old that the verb 'to be' has different uses or senses: the existential, the predicative, and the 'is' of identity. Why should we regard this as a question of central importance to the sciences or as the main, perhaps the only, genuine philosophical question? The scientist can decide *that* certain entities *are* (the existential 'is') and *what* they are (the predicative 'is'). What more does he, or the philosopher, have to do with being? But being is not, Heidegger argues, the thin, unappetizing subject that it has come to seem. To see why this is so we need to look at the 'various meanings of being' that he found in Brentano's book on Aristotle and later in Aristotle himself.

According to Aristotle the verb 'to be' is ambiguous in several dimensions. When we say that something is (such-and-such or a so-and-so), we may mean that it is actually or that it is potentially. (For Aristotle actuality is logically prior to potentiality.) Again, 'to be' is sometimes equivalent to 'to be true, to be the case'. But most importantly the meaning of 'to be' varies with the category of the entity to which it is applied. Aristotle proposed ten categories, of which the most fundamental is substance, while items in the others – quality, quantity, relation, and so on – depend for their being on substances. Everything that there is falls into one or other of these categories, so that they are classes or genera of entities. But they are, on Aristotle's view, the highest genera that there are. Beings as a whole do not constitute a genus, since 'being' is ambiguous: this can most easily be seen, if we consider that a substance, such as a horse, simply *is*, while a quality, such as its brown colour, is the colour *of* the horse, its being depends on that of the substance to which it belongs. An ambiguous or equivocal term cannot demarcate a genus: horses as an animal species, for example, constitute a single genus, but if we take the word 'horse' in its full range of meanings and make it cover rocking-horses, clothes-horses, and vaulting-horses as well as the animals, we no longer have a genuine genus, but a disparate collection of entities united by nothing but an ambiguous noun. The difference between 'horse' and 'being' is that while the different senses of horse are not significantly related to each other, but only by historical contingencies and superficial resemblances the different senses of 'being' are systematically and significantly related to each other, possessing, Aristotle sometimes suggests, a unity of 'analogy'. At all events being, in its various senses, is sufficiently unified to constitute a single topic of enquiry in a way that the various types of 'horse' do not, if not to constitute a genus in the way that horses do.

3. Heidegger in the spring of 1912

Being acquired further accretions and refinements in its later history; it acquired, for example, the medieval distinction between being as essence and being as existence, which does not emerge clearly in Aristotle. But enough has been said to set the stage for Heidegger. He agreed with Aristotle that there were different types of being, if not exactly different senses of 'being'. He introduces for this a third term alongside 'that'-being, the fact *that* something is or exists, and 'what'-being, what that thing is: 'how'-being, the mode, manner, or type of an entity's being. For example, if we remain for the moment within the confines of Aristotle's categories, then we have, first, the fact that horses exist, secondly those features of horse that distinguish it from

17

other animals and from other substances in general, and finally its mode of being, the fact that it is a substance and not an entity in some other category. Or, to take a case that goes beyond the confines of Aristotle's categories, while the mathematician studies the 'what' of numbers, asking such questions as whether every even number is the sum of two primes, the philosopher asks about the being of numbers, about how they are or their way of being (cf. xxii. 8, 43; xx. 149). He may answer, as Husserl did, that numbers are neither physical nor psychological entities, but are 'ideal' rather than 'real' entities. In that case, their mode of being is one of ideality rather than reality.

Heidegger versus Aristotle

If Aristotle and his successors have done so much work on the question of being, what more can Heidegger do? Often he suggests that the philosopher should not accept doctrines that have hardened into dogmas even if they happen to be true; he must return to the source from which the doctrine originally sprang, thinking it through afresh. But such rethinking invariably modifies the inherited doctrine to an extent. And in this case Heidegger takes issue with Aristotle at several points. In particular, Aristotle implies, despite his several categories, that the being of genuinely existent entities is all of a piece, that everything – God, men, plants, animals, statues, and chisels – is a substance with qualities, a quantity, relations, and so on. All entities are regarded as *vorhanden*, 'present at hand', as appropriate objects of disinterested description. Heidegger will argue in BT that not all entities are of this type. A hammer, for example, is properly seen as an object of use, to be described, if at all, as 'too heavy' or 'just right', rather than in terms of its physical dimensions and properties. The token that the lover offers to his beloved is a flower, not a plant, not an object of botanical enquiry. Even philosophers who seem to distinguish between different types of entity reveal on closer inspection that they assimilate the being of these entities to a single pattern. Descartes, for example, distinguished sharply between the *res cogitans*, the thinking thing or substance, and the *res extensa*, the extended thing or substance. But not only does he thereby assimilate the being of tools and that of planets, both being at bottom simply extended things; he also, if less obviously, assimilates the being of the thinking thing with that of the extended thing, for each is a thing with an essential attribute, albeit a different attribute. Might we not say that everything that is or exists is or exists in the same way, that to exist is to be a bearer of predicates (or 'the value of a variable') and that entities that apparently are in different ways simply bear different predicates? But not everything, Heidegger will reply, is a bearer of predicates, and to assume that it is already introduces a surreptitious homogenization of being.

Why do philosophers tend to homogenize the being of entitles? One reason, Heidegger implies, is that they focus on individual entities or types of entity to the exclusion of the context in which they lie. It is, for example, easier to see a hammer as *vorhanden*, as a thing with certain properties or a bearer of predicates, if one ignores the engrossed carpenter hammering in a nail. We need to consider then not simply the being of entities within the world, but the being of their surrounding context, and ultimately the being of the world as a whole. We also need to look at being as such, to see how and why it branches out into different varieties.

Heidegger does not, however, immediately consider either beings as a whole or being as such. He turns to the examination of the human being, Dasein.

Chapter 4
Dasein

Philosophers often have good reason to place the human being at the centre of their enquiry. An epistemologist who asks 'What can I know?' can be expected to say something about the status of the knower. For a phenomenologist such as Husserl, exploring the relationship between, on the one hand, the 'transcendental' ego, subject, or consciousness and, on the other, its objects, the human being is clearly central. (Heidegger often criticizes these philosophers for saying too little about the being of the subject.) But if we are concerned about being and beings, the human being seems to have no privileged status. It is surely simply one being among others. Why should we start with any particular entity, and why Dasein in particular? It is true that Aristotle held that the study of being must begin with an exemplary type of being, namely substance, and with the exemplary instance of that type, namely God. But Heidegger rejected the link between ontology and theology that Aristotle thereby established, and he does not suggest, at any rate explicitly, that Dasein is an exemplary or paradigmatic entity. What he does say is that it is Dasein that asks the question 'What is Being?' But, we interject, any question whatsoever is asked by Dasein. Are we to suppose that to answer, say, the question 'What are the mating habits of giraffes?' we need first to explore the being of the human being who asks the question? In a sense we do. For to ask and to set about answering any question we need a preliminary understanding, however vague, of the subject-matter of the question and of the direction in which the answer is to be sought. In this case, we need at least to know that the meaning of the word 'giraffe' is to be found in a dictionary or encyclopaedia, and we are likely to know even more than that if the question is capable of arousing our interest. Our preliminary understanding of giraffes is, however, not in itself a subject of great interest nor is it, after it has given us initial guidance, of much relevance to the question we have asked.

Likewise Dasein has a preliminary understanding of being. If it did not we could not understand the question 'What is being?' nor begin to set about answering it. Indeed all human beings, even those who do not ask this question, have some understanding of being, otherwise they could not engage with beings, even with themselves. (Heidegger does not consider infants in his published works, but he would doubtless say first that an infant who is capable of learning by interacting with entities must already have some implicit understanding of being, and secondly that we can only understand infancy as a 'privation' of adulthood, by contrast with our understanding of fully fledged Dasein.) Such understanding is not an explicit conceptual account of being, such as the philosopher aspires to, nor need it be a wholly impeccable understanding. It is prone to various types of error. But we cannot, as we can in the case of giraffes, after initially consulting our preliminary understanding at once abandon it to go off in search of the real object of our quest, hoping perhaps to correct any errors in our preliminary understanding by confronting being face to face. For the being of beings is not as localized, as conspicuous, or as independent of ourselves as are the mating habits of giraffes. Being is everywhere: everything is – people, hammers, towns, theories, planets, galaxies. Being is nowhere: it does not inhere in entities as a readily discernible property; if it is to be discerned, we need continuous guidance from our preliminary understanding of being, and, whatever adjustments we may make to it, we can never wholly abandon it for, or test it against, a stark encounter with being itself. The being of beings, of other entities as well as of Dasein itself, is not independent of Dasein: theories, questions, tools, cities – all these depend for their existence, and for their mode of being, on the fact that they are produced, asked, used, inhabited, and interpreted by human beings. Dasein is essentially in the world, not simply in the sense that it occupies a place in the world together with other things, but in the sense that it continually interprets and engages with other entities and the context in which they lie, the 'environment' or the 'world around us'. It is, in a way, only because Dasein does this that there is a unitary world at all rather than a collection of entities. Dasein is not just one thing among others; it is at the centre of the world, drawing together its threads. Thus in selecting Dasein as the starting-point for his enquiry Heidegger does not focus on one type of entity to the exclusion of others; Dasein brings the whole world along with it.

Why 'Dasein'?

'Dasein' is Heidegger's way of referring both to the human being and to the type of being that humans have. It comes from the verb *dasein*, which means 'to exist' or 'to be there, to be here'. The noun *Dasein* is used by other philosophers, by Kant for example, for the existence of any entity. But Heidegger restricts it to human beings. He also stresses the root meaning of the noun, namely 'being there' or 'being here'. *Da* in ordinary German is appropriately translated sometimes as 'there' and sometimes as 'here', depending on the context. (Heidegger occasionally suggests that while 'here' (*hier*) is where I, the speaker, am, and 'there' (*dort*) is where he or she, the person spoken about, is, *da* is where you, the addressee of my remarks, are (xx. 343). But he does not usually think of Dasein as you rather than I) The word *sein* means 'to be' and, as a noun (*Sein*), 'being' in the abstract sense. Sometimes, but not always, Heidegger hyphenates the word, '*Da-sein*', to stress the sense of 'being (t)here'.

Why does he speak of the human being in this way? The being of humans is strikingly different from that of other entities in the world. 'Dasein is an entity for which, in its Being, that Being is an issue' (BT, 191). Unlike other entities, it has no definite essence:

> The essence of Dasein lies in its existence. Accordingly those characteristics which can be exhibited in this entity are not 'properties' present-at-hand of some entity which 'looks' so and so and is itself present-at-hand; they are in each case possible ways for it to be, and no more than that.... So when we designate this entity with the term 'Dasein', we are expressing not its 'what' (as if it were a table, house, or tree) but its Being.
>
> (BT, 42)

That Dasein's being is an issue for it depends, in part, on the fact that this being is 'in each case mine', that Dasein needs to be addressed with a personal pronoun, 'I' or 'you'. The being of entities which are merely present at hand and which are not therefore appropriately addressed as 'I' or 'you' is a matter of indifference to them. Since they cannot, like Dasein, take charge of their own being, they need, if they are to be anything at all, a definite 'what'. But a human being is whatever it decides or has decided to be: 'Dasein is its possibility' (BT, 42). Dasein violates Aristotle's ontology in two respects. First, it is not a substance with an essential nature and with properties or 'accidents'. Second, Dasein's potentiality or possibility is prior to its actuality: Dasein is not a definite actual thing, but the possibility of various ways of being.

'To be or not to be, that is the question'

We naturally think of Hamlet. Dasein is an entity that can decide whether to be or not. But Hamlet does not suggest that a man is nothing more than something that can decide whether or not to be. Why might he not in addition have, like 'a table, house, or tree', some determinate nature? Indeed he must have some further characteristic apart from this ability to decide whether or not to be. Nothing could consist solely in that capacity, any more than it could have existence as its sole characteristic. In any case a man does not have an unrestricted power to decide whether or not to be. He may choose to die, but he cannot choose to be born, or to be born in one situation rather than another. He is, as Heidegger puts it, 'thrown' into the world. But once Dasein is thrown it has more control over its own being than just the option of suicide if it does not like what it is. (Heidegger does not mention suicide in BT, but it is clear from xx. 439 that he regarded it as an inappropriate or 'inauthentic' response to the possibility of death.) What I decide, therefore, is not so much whether or not to be, but how to be. Here we have a different use of expressions such as 'how it is', and 'manner, mode, or way of being'. So far we have assumed that an entity has one, and only one, way of being, but now we see that Dasein's way of being involves the capacity to choose among several possible ways of being. I can choose to be a priest, a doctor, or a philosopher. An appropriate answer to the question 'What am I?' takes the form not of a disinterested comment on myself, but of a decision about how I am to be, even if it is only the confirmation of a decision I have already made. Heidegger marks this special character by saying that Dasein, alone of all entities, *exists* or has *existence*. The verb *existieren* and the noun *Existenz*, like their English equivalents, stem from Latin words meaning literally 'to stand forth' and 'standing forth'. Dasein stands forth, creating its own ways of being, in a way that no other entity does. This feature of Dasein is so crucial that Heidegger decides that instead of speaking of 'categories', as we do when we examine the being of other entities, we should speak rather of 'existentials' (*Existenzialien*), to mark the basic features of Dasein's being (BT, 44).

Is it not an exaggeration to say that Dasein involves no 'what', no 'properties', but consists wholly in its 'possibility'? I may after all be too stupid to become a priest, a doctor, or a philosopher. I may become bald, through no choice of my own and with no possibility of

24

regrowing my hair. Most human beings have a certain bodily, biological structure which differs markedly from that of other creatures and they have only limited possibilities of altering it. Some philosophers have located man's distinctive nature in rationality, defining man as a rational animal. Heidegger does not of course argue that Dasein can become whatever it wants. Circumstances place restrictions on what I can do: 'Existentiality is always determined by facticity' (BT, 192). But my circumstances and my condition are never simply 'present-at-hand properties': I can always respond to them in various ways. If I become bald, I may refuse to accept that I am bald, continuing to insist that I have a full head of hair; I may wallow in my baldness, and let it drive me to despair; I may wear a wig; I may simply ignore it; or I may gladly

4. Heidegger with Manfred Schröter at a conference of the Munich Academy in 1953

accept my baldness, flaunt it, and perhaps make it the basis of a successful career as a lover or an actor. Which option I take is not determined solely by my baldness, but is freely chosen by me.

Inauthenticity and the 'They'

But is it freely chosen by me? The fact that baldness is a significant, and disagreeable, feature of a person requiring some special response depends on social conventions that I did not initiate, and so too does the range of appropriate responses to it. Wearing a wig is an acceptable response, whereas attempting to shave the heads of everyone else so that I am no longer exceptional is not. 'One does not do such things', I think, and in doing so I exclude this as an option, to such an extent that I am unlikely even to consider the possibility. In so far as I refuse or fail to consider certain options for the reason that 'they', 'one', or 'we' do not do such things, my condition is one of 'inauthenticity' rather than 'authenticity', and I have ceded my decision to 'others' or rather to the anonymous 'they'.

Heidegger's word for 'authentic' is *eigentlich*, which in ordinary German means 'real' or 'proper'. From it he forms the word *Eigentlichkeit*, 'authenticity'. 'Inauthentic' is *uneigentlich* – which usually means 'not literal, figurative' and 'inauthenticity' is *Uneigentlichkeit*. Dasein is sometimes authentic and sometimes not. Does Heidegger mean that only authentic Dasein is really Dasein, is really a human being? That inauthentic Dasein is not properly human? No. He associates *eigentlich* with the adjective *eigen*, 'own', which is used in such contexts as 'having a room of one's own', 'having a mind of one's own', and 'being one's own master'. To be authentic is to be true to one's *own* self, to be one's *own* person, to do one's *own* thing.

What then is inauthenticity? Whose mind might I have, whose person might I be, if not my own? 'Own' usually contrasts with '(an)other's', and *eigen* contrasts with *fremd*, 'alien, another's'. I might emulate some other person or group – Heidegger, my spouse, or my academic colleagues – doing and thinking what they do and think. But more often, Heidegger believes, I conform to what the '*they*' does and thinks. Here he exploits a simple German pronoun, *man*, 'one', as in 'One pays one's debts', though English often uses 'we', 'they', 'you, or 'people' where German uses *man*. Heidegger turns this pronoun into a definite noun, *das Man*, the 'one' or the 'they'. The 'they' is others, but it also includes myself in so far as I do, think, and feel what 'they' do, think, and feel. It is not definite named others, it is everyone and no one. I am writing in English, because that is what *one* does. I grieve at funerals because that is what *one* does. In so far as I conform to the 'they', I am not my own individual self, but the '*they-self*': 'The Self of everyday Dasein is the they-self, which we distinguish from the *authentic Self*' (BT, 129). Dasein is inauthentic in so far as it does things simply because that is what *one* does. It is authentic in so far as it makes up its own mind, is its own person, or true to its own self. Authenticity need not of course imply eccentricity. Eccentricity can be inauthentic, while conformity to standard practices can be authentically chosen.

Inauthenticity is by no means an unqualified blemish. It is the normal condition of most of us for most of the time, and without it we could not make decisions at all. I could not decide to write a book, had I not acquired a language such as English. Then, given that my intended audience is anglophone, it does not occur to me to wonder whether I should write it in ancient Greek rather than English, whether to write from left to right or from right to left, or whether to use the word 'good' in the sense of 'bad'. On the other hand, the fact that I am bound to write in English does not commit me to repeating sentences and phrases used by others, 'clichés' and stock expressions; if I do this, without trying to work out my own ideas or to find an apt, if hitherto unused, expression for them, my authenticity is out of place. Still, whether my inauthenticity is inappropriate or not, the question arises: can I, to the extent that I am inauthentic, be said to decide my own being? Heidegger's answer is that if I am inauthentic, if I have ceded my decisions to the 'they', I have, implicitly, decided to do so. At any rate it is always possible for me to reclaim my choice; it is not necessarily very easy to do so, but it is at least possible. And if I can by my decision escape from inauthenticity, then my failure to do so depends on a decision, however implicit, not to make my escape. Dasein's inauthenticity then does not mean that Dasein does not 'exist', dispose, that is, over its own being.

Dasein and the Body

What about the body? Is that not a definite, inescapable 'what' that every human being possesses? My body is not of course only a 'what': I can decide to do many things both with it and to it. But any human being must be embodied and there is a central biological core of the human body that cannot be removed or radically altered, if one is to remain alive. It is clear from Heidegger's account of Dasein that Dasein is embodied, it is not a bare ego or an exclusively psychological subject. But he rarely mentions the body. Suppose then that I attempt to describe the human body. How am I to do it? I might try to describe it in terms which do not essentially imply that it is the body of a living human being who walks, talks, hammers, and so on, in terms that assimilate it to a corpse or to the bodies of other animals. But then, Heidegger objects, if we think of the body in this way, we have to add something to it to make up the complete human being as distinct from a corpse or a nonhuman animal – a soul, for example, or rationality – and then we have lost the unity of the human being, or at least we still have to explain how this unity arises. Again, to regard one's own body in this way is a sophisticated and unnatural procedure. We do not become aware of ourselves, or others, first as extended bodies on a par with stones and rocks, then as living organisms, then as animal bodies, and finally as human beings. We start off, at least in adulthood, viewing ourselves as whole human beings, and need a special sort of abstraction to see ourselves simply as animals or as bodies. The philosopher too, then, should begin by considering Dasein rather than its body, the whole human being who asks the question 'What is my body?' just as it asks the question 'What is being?' When we turn to Dasein, however, we see that we do not normally notice or attend to our own bodies as long as they are in good working order. G. E. Moore once held up his hands and declared 'I know I have two hands'. But we do not usually make such claims about our hands or focus on them at all. We attend to the task in hand, the pen rather than the hand that holds it, or more likely the paper on which we are writing, or more likely still the matters that we are writing about. The body is inconspicuous. It is there, but it lies in the background of Dasein's doings, not in the foreground. It is not something added to Dasein, or to which Dasein is added. Dasein, as Heidegger describes it, essentially requires a body of a certain sort, and is not a soul or ego that might conceivably exist in a disembodied state or in a body quite different from the typical human body. Dasein, its nature and capacities – the software, as it were – is intimately intertwined with its hardware, the body. Nevertheless the software is for Heidegger primary and the hardware secondary.

Dasein and Spirit

Heidegger has good reason for beginning with human beings as Dasein, as questioners, choosers, and self-producers; that is, after all, where we all start from, whether we are biologists, historians, or craftsmen. But, we may object, Dasein is only one aspect of human beings alongside others, not only biology, but also psychology and what German philosophers often call 'spirit' (*Geist*) or the 'spiritual' – sciences, theories, works of art, even the social and political structures we create. Does Heidegger neglect all this? No. They all come in, but only as ways of Dasein's being. Heidegger acknowledges no purely inner psychological realm, nor any ideal realm of logical and mathematical entities. His talk of Dasein's 'being' involves a sturdy realism that demotes, if it does not abolish, such disciplines as logic, psychology, and epistemology. Dasein, even in its deepest moods and emotions, is always engaged with the world and with entities in it. Scientific theories, even the truths of logic and mathematics, are ways of Dasein's being, of its being in the world.

Chapter 5
The World

Heidegger begins by considering Dasein in its 'average everydayness'. Not all of Dasein's capacities are exerted in its average everydayness. It does not make momentous decisions or, on the whole, contemplate its own death. Above all it does not reflect conceptually on its own condition in the way philosophers do. To account for his own ability to do philosophy, even to the extent of reflecting on the everyday condition, Heidegger will have to go beyond average everydayness. But the philosopher is also a human being and, like the rest of humanity, spends much of his time in a state of everydayness. It would be a serious error to describe Dasein as if it were unremittingly engaged in philosophical enquiry. In any case Dasein in its average everydayness shares many characteristics with Dasein in its more elevated modes.

Dasein, whether in its average everydayness or otherwise, is in the world. Stones, trees, cows, and hammers are also in the world. And Dasein too is in the world in the way they are. But Dasein is also in the world in another sense, a sense in which other entities, even cows, are not. Dasein, unlike a stone, a tree, or a cow, is aware of and familiar with the world, aware of other things in the world and of itself, and it is so in virtue of its 'understanding of being'. It is not a self-enclosed subject, aware only of its own mental states. If it were so, it would have a definite 'what' and would neither be, nor need to be, in the world. If Dasein had a determinate nature of its own and were not, at least in part, what it makes of itself, it might not need a world to dwell in. But as things are, Dasein, to be at all or at least to be in its own characteristic ways, needs a world populated with entities for it to engage with.

What is Dasein's world like? It is not for the most part a world of purely natural entities. The most immediate and obvious denizens of Dasein's world, apart from Dasein itself, are the tools and equipment that it uses for its daily needs, its hammer, for example, the nails and the leather with which it makes shoes. Tools and equipment have their place in a workshop, the immediate environing world of Dasein. But this world points beyond itself to a larger world, to the other Dasein who buy the shoes, and to those who supply the leather. This in turn points to nature, not the nature of the natural scientist, but the cows from which the leather comes and the fields in which they graze. Husserl later called this world, the world in which we naturally and normally live, the *Lebenswelt* or 'life-world'. But Heidegger simply called it the world (*Welt*), the wider world beyond the immediate 'world around us' (*Umwelt*), the world of the workplace.

Philosophers have tended to neglect the world in this sense. They assume that the world Dasein inhabits consists of extended natural entities. Descartes, in the first of his *Meditations on First Philosophy*, begins by doubting the reality of the life-world, the fire before him, the cloak wrapped around him, the pen in his hand, and the paper on his lap. When later in the work he overcomes his doubt and restores his belief in the external world, it is the world of mathematical physics, of measurable extended things that wins his assent, not the humble *Umwelt* of the fire, the cloak, the pen, and the paper. But even philosophers who try to give the life-world its due tend to misdescribe it. A phenomenologist such as Husserl, 'abstracting at first from all "significance" predicates and restricting himself purely to the "res extensa"' (CM, 47), describes the experience of seeing a table in the following way. As I walk round a table, it presents to me various visual aspects which, though not identical in shape and colour, are systematically related to each other in such a way that I can, by 'retaining' or remembering the aspects of the table that I have already seen, eventually 'synthesize' them or piece them together to form a conception of the table as it objectively is, a brown rectangular top based on four legs. Heidegger gives, in his early Freiburg lectures on ontology (lxiii. 88–92), a quite different account. What I see is not just *a* table, but *the* table, the table in *this* room. The table is for writing on, or for eating at. I see it as for something. I do not first see it as an extended object and then only later as for something. I hardly take note of the geometrical dimensions of the table or its spatial location with respect to the points of the compass. I see it as well or badly positioned, as, say, too far from the light for reading. I notice scratches on the table, not just interruptions of its uniform colour, but damage done by the children. I think back to the past and recall that it is the table at which we used to discuss politics or at which I wrote my first book.

In this account Heidegger is contemplating a world, or a segment of the world, not actively engaging with it like the craftsman at work. But the two situations exhibit important similarities, as well as differences. First, theoretical cognition is not primarily or even necessarily involved at all. The craftsman does not regard his hammer, and Heidegger does not view the table, as an entity with certain geometrical and physical properties. Both are seen primarily as objects of use, connected to human purposes: the hammer is something for hammering, the table is for eating or writing.

Second, neither the hammer nor the table is seen in isolation from other entities in the setting. The hammer is for hammering in the nails that lie next to it, for working the leather into shoes, and so on. The table is too far from the window, it is where the people I hear outside usually eat, it is where I wrote that book on the shelf. Different entities in the room or the workshop refer to each other, and because they do so they form a significant whole – a complete workshop or room – rather than just a random collection of entities. Objects refer to each other in these ways and thus constitute a realm of 'significance' most obviously and easily if they are objects of use – 'ready to hand', as Heidegger puts it, *zuhanden*, in contrast to entities that are merely present at hand, *vorhanden*. Neither the workshop nor the room is a self-enclosed environment. The workshop and its contents refers beyond itself to customers, cows, and meadows. The room too refers to the carpenter who made the table, the tradesmen who supply food, the publishers who print books, and so on. In each case the immediate world around us points to a larger world beyond, but a world that is still anchored in Dasein, its needs and purposes.

Thirdly, space and time are involved in both situations, but with a different role from that assigned to them by Husserl. Husserl is interested primarily in geometrical shapes, the shapes both of the different perspectival aspects of the table that successively present themselves to us, and of the actual table that we piece together from these aspects. Time for Husserl is primarily our temporal awareness of our experiences of the table. When I first see a table, I experience not the table as a whole but an aspect of it from a particular standpoint. If I have seen a table before, I expect or anticipate that my experiences as I walk round the table will be of a certain sort, I 'protain' my subsequent experiences. As I continue to walk around it, these expectations or 'protentions' are 'fulfilled' by the actual experiences I have. But this would be of little benefit to me if I at once forgot the experiences I had already had, if I did not 'retain' my past experiences as well as have my present one and protain those to come. Retention and protention enable me to be aware of the temporal flow of my experiences and to view them as experiences of an objective table, whose actual shape does not correspond exactly to any single experience of it. For Heidegger, impressed though he was by Husserl's analyses, space and time play a different role. What we naturally notice about the table is not its precise shape and dimensions, but whether it is the right size and in the right place for our purposes. Is it big enough to seat the whole family for a meal? Is it too far from the light or from the bookcase for writing? Objects have their proper positions in the room. So too in the workshop. Nails, leather, hammer are placed within easy reach on the workbench. Through the window the craftsman can see the road that leads, in one direction, to the centre of the town and, in the other, to the next village, where his sister now lives. He does not know the exact distances to these places, but he knows that it is only a short walk to the town centre, while the walk to the next village takes some time and he is usually hungry by the time he gets there. (Peasants in Greece often used to express the distance from one place to another in terms of the number of cigarettes one would smoke on the journey. A village close by was, say, two cigarettes away, while a long walk was a whole packet.) Time too is, for Heidegger, a matter of 'significance'. The table points ahead to the uses that will be made of it, and back to past events – the scratches made by the boys, the book he wrote at it, and so on. The craftsman too, absorbed in his hammering, looks ahead implicitly to the shoe he will have made, to the fresh supply of leather that he needs to order, and back perhaps to his youth when he was taught his skills by his father, from whom he inherited the workshop.

There is, however, an important difference between these two situations. As Heidegger surveys the room he notices the scratches on the table, he explicitly recalls eating, writing, and conversing at the table, and so on. The craftsman, by contrast, when he is engrossed in hammering a nail, does not explicitly notice or attend to the bench he is working on, the stool he sits on, the supply of nails beside him. He need not be thinking about his customers, his suppliers, the cows in the meadow. These things are *there* for him, he is tacitly aware of them, but they are inconspicuous and unobtrusive; he sees them, as it were, out of the corner of his eye and does not focus on them. This is possible because these entities refer to each other and constitute a web of significance. The stool, the bench, the nails beside him, even the hammer itself, remain inconspicuous as long as they are in their proper positions, ready to play their proper part in his task. He will notice them if something goes wrong. If the head of the hammer comes off or the stool collapses they become conspicuous. Or, again, if his leather is missing, runs out, or is not in its proper place, it becomes conspicuous in a way that it was not before.

The same is true of the craftsman himself. Husserl, Heidegger believed, was wrong to say that the 'ego is himself existent for himself in continuous evidence' (CM, 66). When the craftsman is absorbed in his work, he focuses on the nail he is hammering or the shoe he is making. He is barely aware of himself even as an embodied agent, let alone as an 'ego'. He may focus on himself if something goes wrong. But he is otherwise as inconspicuous to himself as the nails beside him or the spectacles on his nose. It has been a persistent mistake of past philosophers to make things too conspicuous: 'when direction on an object is taken as the basic structure of consciousness, being in the world is characterized far too explicitly and sharply' (xvii. 318).

The world, then, and things in the world are normally inconspicuous to everyday Dasein. This raises a problem. Philosophers are not a distinct species from everyday Dasein. How then can they rise above average everydayness to become aware of what everyday Dasein fails to notice? Heidegger regards himself as a phenomenologist in the sense that he makes apparent what is usually inconspicuous, and he does not do so by out-of-the-way experiments or by abstruse arguments. What Heidegger notices, and presents in conceptual garb, is in a way obvious to anyone once it is pointed out to them. But how does he manage to notice it in the first place? Conversely, we may think that what Heidegger has pointed out is radiantly obvious and that the mystery is that any philosopher ever overlooked it. Heidegger has a complex task: he has not only to give an analysis of Dasein and to convince us of its correctness, he has also to explain why he – unlike everyday Dasein – is able to give this account and also why other philosophers, not themselves perpetually enmeshed in everydayness, were not.

Being in the World

Dasein and the world are not two distinct entities that can vary independently of each other. They are complementary. If we regard either in a certain way, this will commit us to regarding the other in a certain way or it will at least exclude certain ways of viewing it. If we regard the world in Descartes's way, as a collection of extended things, then it is natural to view the self as a thinking thing, and, conversely if we view the self as a thinking thing it is natural to view the world it inhabits as consisting of present-at-hand extended things. If we reject this account and view the world as a web of significance, then we are committed to a different view of Dasein. Dasein's approach to the things around it is a practical one of circumspect concern rather than disinterested contemplation. Heidegger does not deny that there are derelict craftsmen who neglect their affairs or that a usually industrious craftsman may have a headache today and feel that he cannot be bothered. Even what we normally regard as a lack of concern is a sort of concern – Dasein never lacks concern in the way that a stone, a tree, or a cow does. But Dasein's attitude is not only practical. The customary distinction between the practical and the theoretical, action and knowledge, is a construct that lies above the level of everyday Dasein. Dasein also knows things. It knows what a hammer is for; it knows how to use it; it knows where the leather is kept; it knows its way around the workshop. It cannot of course say how it knows all this or put its knowledge into words. Some things are easier done than said. But it knows as well as does things. If it did not, there could not be a world in Heidegger's sense. Tools that nobody knows how to use, or ever knew how to use, cannot constitute a web of interreferential significance; they would lie indifferently alongside each other like rocks in an uninhabited desert.

Dasein knows not only the individual items in the workshop and how to use them. It also knows the world and knows its way about in it. What Heidegger has in mind is best illustrated by the sense of direction that enables us to find our way around a familiar town. We cannot easily say how we do it or give explicit directions to a stranger, but we manage to find our own way without difficulty. We do not painfully pick our way along a familiar route by noting the houses and side-streets on the way; we walk straight to our destination, often oblivious of our surroundings along the way. Usually we do it without maps. In fact maps would be of little use to someone who lacked altogether a sense of direction; we need a sense of direction even to find our way around the map and then to orient the map to our immediate environment. Nor is this just an analogy. For Dasein's world is, Heidegger stresses, a spatial world. It is not spatial in the way that Descartes's and Newton's (or even Leibniz's) world is spatial, a world of cold, neutral co-ordinates. It is a world of directions – up–down, left–right, behind–ahead, and North–South–East–West. It is a world where things are near and far, but distances are not measured only in miles or kilometres; what is near as the crow flies may be far if an unbridged river or a trackless mountain lies between, and things that are too close may, like one's spectacles, be too far to be seen. It is a world in which things have their rightful places, not a purely Euclidean world in which an object may occupy any place of the appropriate size.

The *A Priori*

How is such being-in-the-world possible? Is Dasein simply a blank tablet that takes on whatever the world offers to it? Not in Heidegger's view. Since world and Dasein are complementary, features of the world are to be explained in terms of features of Dasein, and the most basic of these features are *a priori*. Much of what Dasein knows is of course learnt fairly late in its career. One Dasein can handle a word-processor and can find its way around the keyboard, but knows little about cricket or the details of a cobbler's workshop. Another knows about cricket or shoemaking, but nothing about word-processors. But we all know, however tacitly and implicitly, about tools and equipment, and what an 'equipmental context' is, what a cricket pitch, a cobbler's workshop, and a writer's study have in common. Even someone from a quite different culture, entirely unfamiliar with our practices and occupations, would if he were transported into our world recognize what he saw as a workshop, and not a mere jumble of entities, even if he knew nothing about the details (xx. 334). Understanding what a tool is, and what a world is in which tools lie, is a part of Dasein's essential understanding of being without which it would not be Dasein.

Or take, again, spatiality. Dasein does not simply read off its sense of direction from the world around it. The world is spatial because Dasein is spatial. A Dasein that finds its way easily round Messkirch or Freiburg cannot of course immediately transfer its skill to Marburg, Berlin, Los Angeles, or the Gobi desert. If transferred to any of these places it will feel disoriented; even though it recognizes individual buildings, streets, or mounds, it cannot find its bearings. But its being disoriented is a mark of its intrinsic spatiality, and soon it will come to orient itself, seeing its new environment in terms of the familiar spatial directions.

Being with Others

Heidegger gives a similar account of our relations with other people. Philosophers, especially though not exclusively those philosophers who, like Husserl, regard a human being as primarily acquainted with its own mental states, present our awareness of others in the following way. First I become aware of my own existence and of other non-human entities. I get to know the shape, appearance, and doings of my own body and I am also aware of the inner experiences I have. Then I notice that there are other entities that are of a similar appearance to myself and behave in broadly similar ways when subjected to similar stimuli. The philosopher then wonders how it is possible – intelligible and justifiable – for me to attribute to these beings inner mental states similar to my own. Is it by empathy? How is empathy possible?

This way of looking at the matter is, Heidegger believes, quite mistaken. It ignores both Dasein's understanding of being and its being-in-the-world. As long as it exists Dasein is 'with others'. It knows what another person is as well as it knows itself, or any other entity. It does not need to inspect the details of a person's physique to discover that it is a person; we are often aware of the presence of others, of what they are doing and of their attitude towards us, without being aware of the details of their appearance. Even when there are no other people around – the workshop is empty, for example, or the desert is uninhabited – others are conspicuous by their absence: 'Even Dasein's being alone is being-with in the world' (xx. 328). Heidegger is not simply describing the phenomenal character of our experience of others. He is, he believes, describing a structural feature of Dasein. Dasein alone is incomplete, it has no nature of its own in which to bask, but has to decide how to be. But then virtually everything Dasein does or is cries out for others, as suppliers of its raw materials, as purchasers of its products, as hearers, or as readers. Dasein's world is essentially a public world, accessible to others as well as itself.

Moods

Heidegger does not speak in such cases as these of Dasein's knowledge. The term 'knowledge' suggests something altogether too explicit and theoretical. He speaks rather of 'understanding' – understanding how to do things, the world, other people, and, in general, understanding of being. But before explaining what understanding is, he turns to *moods*.

Moods are often supposed to be mental things, inner feelings that play at best a subdued role in our engagement with the world. But that is not how Heidegger sees them. To be in a certain mood is to view the world in a certain way, and it crucially affects our engagement with the world and the ways in which we respond to entities within it. Moods differ from emotions. Emotions concern particular entities. I am angry about something and usually with someone. But if I am in an irritable mood, I need not be irritable about anything in particular, though I am more likely to get angry about particular things than I usually do. If moods are directed at anything they are directed at the world rather than at entities in the world. Anxiety, objectless *Angst*, or boredom (to take Heidegger's examples) cast a pall over the world, in contrast to fear in the face of a specific threat or boredom with some specific thing, such as the minister's speech. Moods are hardly within our control. I can control my deeds, decide what to do, and restrain myself from doing what I have an urge to do. To a degree I can control my emotions: I can refrain from insulting the object of my anger, and I can turn my thoughts to something else to get my anger to die down. But moods come and go as they please, unresponsive to our direction. Since they do not concern specific entities, I cannot remove the pall of depression by manipulating specific entities; every specific entity to which I turn my attention lies under the same pall. Heidegger expresses this by using an unusual word: *Befindlichkeit*, which means roughly 'how one finds oneself', 'how one is to be found', or 'how one is doing', but is often misleadingly translated as 'state of mind'. The more usual German word for mood, *Stimmung*, also means the 'tuning' of a musical instrument, and Heidegger also exploits this association: to be in a mood is to be tuned or attuned in a certain way.

But are moods as significant as Heidegger supposes them to be? Most of us, for most of the time, are in no definable mood, and even if we are in a bad mood we go about our normal business in much the same way as when we are in a good mood. But what is our normal business? Why, to take the example discussed above, is Heidegger looking at the table and the room in which it lies rather than getting down to business, in the way that the craftsman does in his workshop? Is it because he is alone in the house? No. There may be people in the next

The World

41

room engaged in heated conversation or a game of cards. Even if he is alone, he could take the opportunity to read a book or draft a plan for writing one. Is it that he understands more or less than the others do about his surroundings? No. The craftsman and the others in the house understand as much as Heidegger does in the relevant sense. They too sometimes survey their surroundings, though they do not describe them as aptly as Heidegger does. It must be because Heidegger is in a mood of, say, pensive nostalgia. He is not in the mood for conversation, cards, reading, or writing. He may of course be snapped out of his present mood if the others cajole him or he may steel himself to engage in these activities in the face of his mood. But not all moods are so easily dispelled or overridden:

> I walked to a neighbouring town; and sat down upon a settle in the street, and fell into a very deep pause about the most fearful state my sin had brought me to; and, after long musing, I lifted up my head; but methought I saw as if the sun that shineth in the heavens did grudge to give me light; and as if the very stones in the street, and tiles upon the houses, did band themselves against me. Me thought that they all combined together to banish me out of the world. I was abhorred of them, and unfit to dwell among them, because I had sinned against the Saviour. Oh, how happy now was every creature over I for they stood fast, and kept their station. But I was gone and lost.
>
> John Bunyan, *Grace Abounding*

But few of us, it may be objected, are in such a disabling mood for long. Can we not ignore such unusual moods as peripheral to being in the world? Even if we could, it would not follow that moods as such are unimportant. For if the busy craftsman or the pensive Heidegger are not, and cannot be, in such a mood as Bunyan describes, they must be in some other mood. Dasein is never moodless, any more than it is ever unconcerned. To be in the average, everyday, apparently moodless condition is itself to be in a mood, albeit a mood for which we have no ready term or brief description. The music that is often essential for

5. Heidegger with Georges Braque, Varengeville, 1955

disclosing the world of a film conveys the *mood* of the film – contentment, excitement, anxious expectancy, or average everydayness. But it is only in films that moods need music. We bring our own moods to the world without special aids.

Is it right, in any case, to call Bunyan's mood disabling? While it lasts it prevents us from making shoes, writing books, from engaging in either the humdrum routine of life or in making crucial decisions. It is not what we normally regard as an appropriate response to any sin that most of us, least of all Bunyan himself, have committed. Most of us are glad to be free of such moods. But most of us are not philosophers of Heidegger's stature and dedication. For, Heidegger believes, moods such as this reveal things that we are usually unaware of. They light up the world and our being in the world in a way that everyday business does not. The craftsman catches a glimpse of his world, of the worldly character of his world, when he finds a tool missing; he notices the

43

whole in the conspicuously absent part. But a mood such as Bunyan's discloses the world more forcibly and memorably: it reveals the worldliness of the world and, by contrast, the everyday unobtrusiveness of the world. Heidegger believes that such moods (or at least less extreme cases such as boredom and *Angst*) are a vital source of insight for the philosopher. But they are not of course the exclusive preserve of the philosopher. Unphilosophical, everyday Dasein is prone to them too, and so moods play a part in Heidegger's attempt to explain how Dasein becomes a philosopher.

Moods alone, however, do not disclose the world. For this we need understanding.

Understanding

Everyday Dasein understands the world, things in the world, and itself. Here again we see a connexion between everyday Dasein and the philosopher. For Heidegger too wants to understand and interpret Dasein, the world, and their being. (He speaks in the introduction to BT of his enterprise as hermeneutic, that is, interpretative – somewhat like, though not exactly like, the interpretation of a text.) Heidegger's enterprise is a continuation of what Dasein does every day. But it is not simply a continuation of it. For Heidegger wants to give a conceptual account of what he understands, while everyday Dasein understands only preconceptually. Its understanding is not the same as theoretical cognition. On the contrary, cognition presupposes a prior understanding of what we wish to know, in much the way that Heidegger's attempt to give a conceptual account of the meaning of being presupposes a prior *understanding* of Being. Understanding, then, is not something that contrasts with other approaches to things, such as knowing about them or explaining them. It is presupposed by them all, since it in part constitutes our being-in-the-world.

What Dasein understands is not so much any particular item in its environment, as its environment as a whole and its own place in it. But Dasein does not simply understand its environment as one might understand an alien text or culture from which one is entirely disengaged. It understands it as presenting to it a range of possibilities. If it did not understand it in this way it could not understand its environment as 'significant'. Although Heidegger speaks of understanding's 'projection' of Dasein on its possibilities, he has in mind nothing so definite and deliberate as a 'project' or plan, but simply that 'as long as it is, Dasein always has understood itself and always will understand itself in terms of possibilities' (BT, 145). The shoemaker sees his workshop as a field of possibilities for him, and is perhaps wondering what to do next. Even the carefree sunbather understands himself in terms of the possibilities of continuing to lie where he is, taking a dip in the sea, or going to refill his glass. Dasein is 'constantly more than it factually is' (BT, 145), always (unless it is asleep) poised between alternative possible ways of continuing. Man is not a passive creature, roused to activity only by external stimuli; he is constantly up to something.

Interpretation

Somewhat more explicit than understanding is interpretation, which in German (*Auslegung*) also means 'laying out'. What I interpret is not so much my environment as a whole, but specific items within it, and also myself. I interpret something as something, as a hammer for example, and I do so primarily in terms of what it is for, in this case banging in nails. Although interpretation does not focus on the environment as a whole, it presupposes an understanding of it. I cannot interpret something as a hammer unless I already understand something about nails, wood, and so on. Similarly I cannot understand something as a hammer unless I have a prior general understanding of what tools and equipment are. Heidegger insists that when I interpret something as a hammer I do not first see the entity as simply present at hand, as a length of wood with a piece of iron attached to it, and then interpret

45

this as a hammer. I implicitly understand it as *zuhanden*, as equipment, from the start:

> In interpreting, we do not, so to speak, throw a 'signification' over some naked thing which is present-at-hand, we do not stick a value on it; but when something within-the-world is encountered as such, the thing in question already has an involvement which is disclosed in our understanding of the world, and this involvement is one which gets laid out by the interpretation.

(BT, 150)

Any interpretation involves, on Heidegger's view, a 'fore-having' (*Vorhabe*), a 'fore-sight' (*Vorsicht*), and a 'fore-conception' (*Vorgriff*) (BT, 150). The interpreter has in advance the, object of his interpretation; Heidegger, for example, has a preliminary understanding of Dasein, before he begins to interpret it. He views the object in a certain way; Heidegger views Dasein with regard to its being. He has preconceptions, concepts in terms of which he proposes to interpret the object; Heidegger will interpret Dasein with such concepts as 'existence'. All interpretation, from the everyday to the philosophical, involves such a 'fore-structure'.

Chapter 6
Language, Truth, and Care

Interpretation need not be expressed in language. I am most likely to make my interpretation of something explicit, if it is broken, malfunctioning, initially unavailable, or needs to be explained to a novice. But language emerges from interpretation and the meanings or significations that it lays out: 'To significations, words accrue' (BT, 161). Words and the entities they apply to are not two disparate realms: words essentially refer to entities and, conversely, entities are essentially meaning-laden and thus give rise to words. The basic form of language is, on Heidegger's view, *Rede*, talk or discourse. Talk is to someone about something. But it need not involve only, or indeed any, assertions; questions, orders, and so on may disclose the world as well as assertions. It need not involve grammatically complete utterances: 'Too heavy – the other one!' is perfectly good talk. Silences are as much a part of talk as are spoken sounds: someone hands me another hammer, he need not bother to explain 'No, not that one – try this instead!' Assertions emerge from talk. Instead of saying 'Too heavy – the other one!, I say 'The hammer is too heavy', and eventually 'The hammer is heavy'. Talk becomes increasingly detached from concrete speech situations in the workplace. A hammer is seen no longer as ready-to-hand, as a tool to be used or rejected, and in its place alongside other tools, but as present-at-hand, as a bearer of properties severed from its involvements with other tools. We end up by taking such a sentence as 'Snow is white', which occurs more commonly in

47

logic textbooks than in down-to-earth talk, as a paradigm of significant discourse. Such assertions are seen as the locus of truth. They are true if, and only if, they correspond to the facts or to some such entity within the world.

Truth

One of Heidegger's most striking doctrines is his rejection of this view of his truth. Truth, he claims, is unconcealment or uncovering. Dasein itself is the primary locus of truth: 'there is truth only in so far as Dasein is and as long as Dasein is' (BT, 227). He does not of course condemn or forgo the making of assertions; they are an essential part of the philosopher's repertoire. An assertion such as 'The hammer is heavy' involves three aspects (BT, 154ff.). First, it points out something, the hammer. It points it out as a hammer and is thus related to the 'as' of interpretation. But the hammer is now a present-at-hand thing, detached from its involvements with its environment. Second, it predicates something, heaviness, of the hammer. Third, it communicates this to another. Why then are assertions not the primary locus of truth?

An assertion is true, it is suggested, if, and only if, it corresponds to a fact. This gives Heidegger two reasons for disputing the theory. For if the theory is correct, there must first be an assertion to correspond to a fact and secondly a fact for it to correspond to. But neither of these items can fill the role assigned to it by the theory. What, first, is an assertion? A string of words perhaps. Or a series of ideas in the mind of the speaker that is then conveyed to the hearer. Or an ideal, logical entity, a timeless proposition. But each of these types of entity – word-sounds, ideas, and propositions – are artificial constructs imposed on the primitive speech situation by a specialized way of looking at the assertion as itself something present-at-hand; none of them naturally present themselves to the normal speaker and hearer. I do not assert something of the idea of a hammer nor does my hearer take the assertion to be about an idea. I am generally not aware of the precise words I utter, let alone the sounds I make. Nor does my hearer hear words as such; he turns to the hammer and its heaviness, and may have some difficulty in recalling my exact words. In any case words already have meanings and thus implicitly involve the entities to which they allegedly correspond. If assertions are to be genuinely independent of the facts and capable of either corresponding to them or failing to do so, we should regard them perhaps simply as sounds. But we do not, Heidegger says, hear pure sounds:

> What we first hear is never noises or complexes of sounds, but the creaking wagon, the motor-cycle. We hear the column on the march, the north wind, the woodpecker tapping, the fire crackling. It requires a very artificial and complicated frame of mind to hear a pure noise . . . Likewise, when we are explicitly hearing the discourse of another, we proximally understand what is said, or – to put it more exactly – we're already with him, in advance, alongside the entity which the discourse is about . . . Even in cases where the speech is indistinct or in a foreign language, what we proximally hear is unintelligible words, and not a multiplicity of tone-data.
>
> (BT, 163f.)

Might words have meanings independent of the things they apply to and refer to, so that we can say that what corresponds to a fact is a meaningful sentence or a proposition? No. A word such as 'hammer' or 'culture' does not have a single determinate meaning or connotation; its meaning depends on, and varies with, the world in which it is used. He expresses this dramatically in his Nietzsche lectures:

> The life of actual language consists in multiplicity of meaning. To relegate the animated, vigorous word to the immobility of a univocal, mechanically programmed sequence of signs would mean the death of language and the petrifaction and devastation of Dasein.
>
> (N i. 144; cf. xxiv. 280f.)

49

There is no pre-packaged portion of meaning sufficiently independent of the world and of entities within it to correspond, or fail to correspond, to the world. Words and their meanings are already world-laden.

If we turn in the other direction and look for chunks of the world to which assertions might correspond, such as the heavy hammer, again we fail to find them. The hammer is entwined in involvements with other entities and has its place in a world. All this is implicitly known to the maker of an assertion and his hearer; otherwise they could not assert, hear, or understand. This world is not disclosed primarily by assertions, but by Dasein's moods and understanding. Dasein then is the primary locus of truth.

Is Heidegger Telling the Truth?

Heidegger makes assertions. He asserts for example that assertion is not the primary locus of truth. Is that assertion, and the others he makes, true? Is the theory that he rejects, and others like it, false? If so, in what sense are Heidegger's assertions true and those of his opponents false? Falsity is not for Heidegger co-ordinate with truth, as it is for those who locate both primarily in assertions. If I assert 'The hammer is heavy' and you say 'No, the hammer is not heavy', one of us is asserting a falsehood. But for this to be possible both of us must agree that there is a hammer there and, more generally, inhabit the same world. Falsehood is only possible against a background of truth and of agreement about the truth. Nevertheless there are falsehoods. But Heidegger does not see them as consisting in the failure of a sentence to correspond to reality. It is more a matter of covering things up, of distorting them, and this may be done in other ways than by making false assertions, by omission or by non-verbal actions. (As Macaulay said: 'A history in which every particular incident may be true may on the whole be false.') Truth by contrast consists in uncovering things. It consists in illuminating things or shedding light on them. It is a matter of degree, of more and less, rather than of either–or. Illumination is never complete, nor ever wholly absent. (Cf. xxvi. 95: 'every philosophy, as a human thing, intrinsically fails; and God needs no philosophy'.) Thus Heidegger rarely speaks of his own views as true and those of his opponents, by contrast, as false. The light he casts reaches only so far, and his opponents are never, and never leave us, wholly in the dark. More often he describes his opponents' views as insufficiently 'original' or 'primordial' (*ursprünglich*), in the sense that they do not get close enough to the 'source' (*Ursprung*) or the bottom of things. Such light as they shed does not reach far enough. They may of course also cover things up, not only by showing things in a false light but also by casting light in the wrong direction.

Heidegger refrains from condemning his opponents' views as false for another reason. Dasein is in (the) truth. Otherwise it could not be in the world. But it is also in untruth. Not only because beings have to be uncovered or illuminated by Dasein and are only ever imperfectly so, but because Dasein has an essential tendency to misinterpret both itself and other beings. A philosopher is also Dasein and is thus prone to the same misinterpretations. Philosophical mistakes are not sheer mistakes; philosophers go wrong because Dasein goes wrong. Philosophers' mistakes disclose a fundamental feature of Dasein.

Falling

Why does Dasein go wrong? Apparently for a variety of reasons. Because Dasein is primarily engrossed in things in the world, it tends to regard itself as a thing, as *zuhanden* or, more likely, as *vorhanden* in the way that the things it deals with are. (Heidegger calls this the 'ontological reflection back of world understanding onto Dasein-interpretation' (BT, 16).) For the same reason, it tends to overlook the obvious, what is too close to be conspicuous, not only its own nature, but its own being-in-the-world, in contrast to the entities it deals with. Again, Dasein submits to the power of the 'they', it does, says, feels, and thinks things simply because that is what 'they' do, say, feel, or think. Related to this is the philosopher's, but not only the philosopher's, tendency to succumb to tradition, to accept inherited concepts, doctrines, and ways of looking at things without subjecting them to adequate independent scrutiny. Heidegger groups these apparently distinct ways of going wrong under the heading of *Verfallen*, 'falling', falling away from oneself into the world.

In BT falling is introduced by way of an account of the further career of assertion. Assertions are essentially communicable to others. The originator of the assertion makes it in the presence of the entities that the assertion is about. But as the assertion is passed on from one person to another, it is accepted by people who are unfamiliar with the original evidence for it, but who accept it and pass it on to others simply because it is what 'they' say. Talk (*Rede*) has become idle talk or chatter (*Gerede*). A close relative of chatter is curiosity, the German word for which, *Neugier*, means literally 'lust for novelty'. The inquisitive chatterbox is constantly on the lookout for the latest news. One sees and reads what 'one' or 'they' has to have seen and read. Chatter and curiosity give rise to ambiguity or duplicity – the German *Zweideutigkeit* has both meanings. When everyone chatters about everything there is no way of telling who really understands what – except perhaps that someone who is really onto something does not chatter about it. Questions are presented as settled when they are really open. But ambiguity and duplicity also infects our relations with one another: 'Under the mask of "for-one-another", an "against-one-another" is in play' (BT, 175). All this, and more, stems from falling:

> Dasein is proximally and for the most part alongside the 'world' of its concern. This 'absorption in . . .' has mostly the character of Being-lost in the publicness of the 'they'. Dasein has, in the first instance, always already fallen away from itself as an authentic ability to be its Self, and has fallen into the 'world'. 'Fallenness' into the 'world' means an

> absorption in Being-with-one-another, in so far as the latter is guided
> by idle talk, curiosity, and ambiguity.

(BT, 175)

To say that Dasein has fallen away from itself is not to say that it was once in an unfallen condition. Dasein has *always already* fallen from itself into the world in something like the way in which I have *always already* paid income tax and never received my gross salary (nor would I receive exactly *that* gross salary if there were no such thing as income tax).

Heidegger's account of falling is vivid and compelling, but it raises several doubts. He now insists that our condition of average everydayness is one of fallenness and inauthenticity. But how can it plausibly be said of the craftsman in his workshop that his life is guided by chatter, curiosity, and ambiguity? This may be true of journalists and their readers, of consumers of culture, and of philosophers. The honest craftsman may retail gossip about matters beyond his expertise, be curious about his neighbours' affairs and make double edged remarks to them. But it is not essential to the everyday pattern of his life and work that he should do such things. Why then is falling an indispensable component of his being? For two reasons. The craftsman is, first, 'proximally and for the most part' absorbed in his daily tasks and does not, except occasionally, step back to survey his life and situation as a whole. Secondly, the world in which he works is a public, not a private, world. It derives its meaning from others, or rather from the anonymous 'they', not from himself alone. He makes shoes of such and such a type because this is what *they* require. He makes them of leather and with a hammer because this is how *one* makes shoes and these are among the socially assigned uses of hammer and leather. All of this is very reasonable; there is, as far as he knows, no better way to make shoes, and given that he is a competent cobbler with a market for his products it would be foolish of him to turn his hand to another trade. (He might use his hammer to crush a rival's skull, but this would make him no more authentic nor elevate him out of fallenness. For murder too is a socially recognized use of a hammer, though one that is generally disapproved of.) This is Dasein's everyday condition and it is, in Heidegger's view, but a few steps away from chatter, curiosity, and ambiguity.

What is wrong with fallenness and inauthenticity? At one level there is nothing wrong with them. They are inevitable features of the human predicament; we cannot step outside our own condition to assess it by an external standard. At another level Heidegger believes that they lead to error. Absorption in the world, or rather in things within the world, leads us to regard ourselves as present at hand, as a thinking thing, as a tool, a machine, or a computer. Our addiction to chatter leads us to detach the assertion from its moorings in worldly significance and view it as an autonomous 'judgement'. Dasein's understanding of being is, in these respects, an unreliable guide. But these errors themselves are not necessarily imposed on us by the chatter of the 'they'. 'They' may say that men are machines and that assertions are 'judgements', but that is a distinct source of error. If we believe that men are machines (or 'subjects') because that is the model that most conspicuously presents itself to us in our dealings with the world, we do not need 'them' to tell it to us too. Conversely, what 'they' say may be correct. It may be ignoble and stunting simply to accept what 'they' say. It may not befit the philosopher's calling to confine his attention to the doctrines, or at least to the problems, retailed at conferences and in recent journals, but the problems may be the right ones and the solutions correct. In any case, the great philosophers of the past – Aristotle, Descartes, Kant – went astray too. Yet surely they were no less authentic, no less resistant to the allure of chatter and the 'they', than Heidegger himself. Heidegger seems to conflate the truth of a person's beliefs with the 'authenticity' of the person himself and of his attachment to the beliefs. He is not the first to do so. Plato too held that philosophy is not simply an effective instrument for acquiring knowledge, but a supremely valuable way of life that, so to speak, opens up the eye of one's soul to the truth.

Fallenness and Truth

Heidegger can be defended on some of these charges if we recall his account of truth. Truth is uncovering and uncoveredness, shedding light and light shed. Someone who simply accepts and passes on the current chatter, even if the chatter happens to be in some sense correct, sheds no light of his own. A great philosopher, by contrast, sheds light even If his views are mistaken. Such errors as he makes are likely, Heidegger believes, to stem from his having taken over something of the tradition without adequate inspection. But in any case the thought of great philosophers is never flatly false. It is never solidified into something simply false or simply true; it is always, as Heidegger said of himself, 'on the way', in transit, never at its destination. It always sheds enough light to guide us in the right direction, even if that leads away from the philosopher himself. Chatter does not do that. Chatter is inert and self-enclosed. It 'tranquillizes' us into thinking that matters are entirely settled and disinclines us to look further.

Heidegger does not simply reject the views of his opponents. He wants to show that philosophers' errors derive from an essential feature of Dasein itself, its fallenness. To do this, he argues that everyday Dasein, exemplified by the craftsman engrossed in his work, is prone to the same failings as the philosopher, that the mistakes made by philosophers are only refined, conceptual versions of everyday misunderstandings. As we shall see in the next chapter, he regards Aristotle's account of time, time as an endless sequence of 'nows' or instants, not only as the general Greek view of time, but as the 'vulgar' or 'ordinary' concept or understanding of time: 'This ordinary way of understanding [time] has become explicit in an interpretation precipitated in the traditional concept of time, which has persisted from Aristotle to Bergson and even later' (BT, 17f.). Why should we agree that the philosopher's concept of time or of, say, the self is already implicit in everyday Dasein's preconceptual understanding of these matters? An unphilosophical craftsman clearly does not think, in conceptual terms, that he is a thing on a par with other things or that time is a sequence of nows. These ideas have never occurred to him and it is not likely that he would assent to them immediately even if they were presented to him. Why should we say that he implicitly understands himself as a thing and time as a sequence of nows? At one level everyday Dasein's understanding of being must, Heidegger believes, correspond closely to Heidegger's conceptual account of it. The craftsman would not be able to do his job properly and find his way around in the world, if he understood himself *exclusively* as, say, a machine, and time *exclusively* as a sequence of nows, rather than as, say, time *to do* things. If that were so, everyday Dasein would be wholly deluded, offering no clues to the meaning of being or, at least, no more clues than the texts of Aristotle and Descartes. But how could that be so? It would defy belief for Heidegger to suggest that he alone of all human beings can get being straight when everyone else is wholly deluded about it. Heidegger is himself Dasein, as were Aristotle and Descartes. He needs some clue to guide him to a conceptual account of being, and if it is not to be just his own peculiar private understanding of it, which could guide him only to his own peculiar private concept of it, it must be an understanding which he shares, in large measure, with others. Everyday Dasein cannot then be wholly deluded in its understanding of being. But can its understanding of being be, at the preconceptual level, impeccably correct? If it were so, how could we explain the fact that philosophers, when they attempt to conceptualize this understanding, so often get it wrong? If philosophers get things wrong, then at some level everyday Dasein must get them wrong. To suggest otherwise is to make philosophers a breed apart, their theories unrelated to everyday Dasein's (and their own) preconceptual understanding of being, though with some affinity to the gossip of non-philosophical chatterers. So all of us, he argues, are fallen. Otherwise the mistakes made by philosophers would be inexplicable.

The Jargon of Authenticity?

In 1964 Theodor Adorno published an attack on Heidegger entitled *The Jargon of Authenticity*. The complaint embodied in the title is one that Heidegger can appreciate. Jargon is a form of chatter, and Heidegger dislikes chatter, the reiteration of statements severed from the context of thought, feeling, and perception that originally gave rise to them. Are we then to accept Heidegger's own philosophy, to adopt it as our own, and to pass it on to others? Presumably not. That would be chatter and inauthenticity. Are we to follow Heidegger's words only until we have been roused to authenticity and then embark on a philosophical quest of our own? No – that sounds like curiosity, hunger for the new. What we should do is perhaps this: spurred to authenticity by our encounter with Heidegger, we should treat Heidegger as he treated Aristotle, Descartes, or Kant, interpreting and disentangling his work, using it as a basis for new thoughts of our own. (Heidegger describes his approach to other philosophers in various ways: as interpretation, as *Destruktion* – a close relative of Derrida's 'deconstruction' – as 'repetition', and, later, as 'conversation'.)

Care

Dasein has so far displayed a variety of features. Heidegger defines its average everydayness as: 'Being-in-the-world which is falling and disclosed, thrown and projecting, and for which its ownmost ability-to-be is an issue, both in its Being alongside the "world" and in its Being-with-others' (BT, 181). No one of these features is basic or 'primordial', in such a way that the rest are derived from it or secondary additions to it. Being alongside the 'world' (that is, dealing with non-human entities within the world) is not prior to being-with-others (that is, interacting with other people). Nor, conversely, is being-with-others primary and being alongside tools, and so on, a secondary feature derived from it. Or again, neither understanding nor mood, 'state-of-mind', is primary; both are equally involved in our disclosure of the world and of ourselves. They are, as Heidegger puts it, equally original or 'equiprimordial'. On the other hand, these features are not separable from each other. There could not be an entity that was alongside the 'world' but not with others, or that was with others but not alongside the 'world'. No being could have understanding but no mood, or mood but no understanding. And so on.

How can we bring unity into this account of Dasein? We can do so, if we regard all these features as rooted in Dasein's basic state of care (*Sorge*). *Sorge*, like 'care', ordinarily has two senses: first, 'caring, worrying' about something, and, secondly, 'taking care' of things. 'Care', as Heidegger uses the word, involves both these senses, but its meaning is more fundamental than either. Even one who is, in the ordinary senses of the words, uncaring, carefree, or careless, is, in Heidegger's sense, caring or careful. It is because Dasein's being-in-the-world is care that we can speak of its concern (*Besorgen*) about the ready-to-hand, such as shoes and hammers, and its solicitude (*Fürsorge*) for other people. But again concern and solicitude are compatible with neglect, contempt, and hatred; the only entities that lack care, concern, and solicitude are those that are wholly incapable of them, such as stones, trees, and animals. Care is distinct from specific attitudes such as willing, wishing, striving, or knowing. To will, wish, or strive for anything whatsoever one must in advance already care. One must care in order to acquire knowledge. In extreme depression or anxiety, the closest that we come in our waking state to lacking care, we find it hard to will or to wish for anything, even for release from our condition.

Although care embodies Dasein as a whole, it is still complex. Heidegger defines it as: 'ahead-of-itself-Being-already-in-(the-world) as

Being-alongside (entities encountered within-the-world)' (BT, 192). Care thus involves three constituents which we have already encountered before. *Dasein is ahead of itself*. It is its possibilities, it is, in a subdued sense, wondering what to do next; it is up to something. Heidegger associates this closely with 'existence', with 'understanding', and also, as we shall see in the next chapter, with the future. *Dasein is already in the world*. This is associated with 'thrownness' and 'facticity' – the fact that Dasein is 'always already' in a specific situation that determines the possibilities available to it – with the mood or 'state of mind' that reveals its thrownness, arid, as we shall see, with the past. *Dasein is alongside entities within the world*. It is engaged in a task, hammering, say, or simply day-dreaming. Heidegger associates this with fallenness, and, as we shall see, with the present. The notion of care thus embraces and reintegrates what we have so far learned about Dasein, and also implicitly points ahead to Dasein's temporal nature. Care is correlative to the significance of the world. Only if Dasein is care can it dwell in a significant world, and only if it dwells in a significant world can Dasein be care.

The Scandal of Philosophy

Heidegger concludes the first division of BT with a discussion of the question whether the external world is real or not. Or rather he rejects the question: the 'scandal of philosophy' is not, as Kant supposed, its failure to give a proof of the reality of things outside me, but the fact 'that such proofs are expected and attempted again and again' (BT, 205). There are two connected flaws in the question. First, it involves an inadequate view of Dasein, of that to which things or the 'world' are supposedly external. Second, it involves an inadequate view of the being of things and of the world. Take Dasein first. Where does the boundary lie between Dasein and what is external to it? Between my body and its environment? Plainly not, at least for the purposes of this question. It is of no philosophical interest to show that there are things outside my own body; once grant that my body exists, and you have granted that there is an external world. Between me and the world, then, with my body counted as something external to me rather than intrinsic to me? Then I am conceived as a pure, 'worldless subject'. And this must be a knowing subject, rather than an acting subject, a subject whose only access to the world is by way of internal states of itself – impressions, ideas, or whatever. But this is not what I am like. My being is care: I potter around doing things in a familiar environment, I am essentially in the world. My access to the world and to things in it is not mediated by ideas or anything of that sort: I hear the 'creaking wagon', not 'pure sounds' (BT, 163), I see trees, not ideas.

The second flaw in the question about the reality of the external world is this. If my being is care and I am essentially in the world, then it cannot be right to regard the world or things in it simply as real or 'present-at-hand'. Viewing the world as real is a secondary, derivative way of viewing it, corresponding to the view of Dasein as a bare, worldless subject. The world is a significant field for my careful involvements with it, not a collection of 'external objects'. Things within the world are primarily ready to hand, equipment for our use.

A World without Dasein?

But this is not the end of the story. I might not have existed. What then? Not much. Things would have gone on much as they do now. But Dasein too might not have existed, there might have been no human beings at all, as there were once presumably no human beings (BT, 227; cf. xxvi. 216). What would there be in such a 'world'? There would be *beings*, but no *being*:

> Entities are, quite independently of the experience by which they are disclosed, the acquaintance in which they are discovered, and the grasping in which their nature is ascertained. But Being 'is' only in the

> understanding of those entities to whose Being something like an
> understanding of Being belongs.
>
> (BT, 183; cf. xxvi. 194)

Without Dasein there would be no being. There would be no truth;
even Newton's laws would not be true, true that is in Heidegger's
sense (BT, 227). There would be no 'world'. But there would be beings
or entities, beings without being. Perhaps Heidegger means that they
would have no specific mode of being. They could not, obviously
enough, have Dasein's mode of being. Nor could they be *zuhanden*,
ready to hand like equipment. Might they not be present at hand, like
rocks and trees? No. Again, this is a way, albeit a secondary and
derivative way, in which Dasein understands things. Even being of this
sort involves disclosure, truth.

Might beings without being be more or less as scientists describe
them, non-significant collections of particles? But a scientist is himself
Dasein, with all the features and limitations that Dasein usually has,
'thrown' into a situation which he cannot escape. Can we be sure that
the discoveries (or as Heidegger would say, 'projections') he makes
from within this situation accurately record what a world without
Dasein would be like? In this spirit R. G. Collingwood quotes J. W. N.
Sullivan as saying: 'The second law of thermodynamics is only true
because we cannot deal practically with magnitudes below a certain
limit. If our universe were populated by intelligent bacteria they would
have no need of such a law' (*The Idea of Nature* (OUP, 1945), 24 n. 1).
And Collingwood adds: 'an intelligent organism whose life had a longer
time-rhythm than man's might find it not so much unnecessary as
untrue' (ibid. 26). Heidegger's response to science is similar, though
not exactly similar. He regards science as a secondary phenomenon,
only one of Dasein's ways of being, derivative from and irretrievably
dependent on other, more everyday ways of being. Even the scientist
uses equipment and knows his way around the laboratory. But suppose
we were to agree, contrary perhaps to Heidegger's own view, that

science gives a fair account of what beings would be like in the absence of Dasein, what would follow from that? We could then say:

1. In the absence of Dasein, things – such as rocks or trees – would be no more than collections of molecules.

Perhaps we would go on to say:

2. Even in the presence of Dasein, things – such as rocks, trees, or hammers – are collections of molecules.

But we might hesitate to say:

3. Things such as hammers are, even in the presence of Dasein, no more than collections of molecules.

Or:

4. Things, such as hammers, are really (in themselves, at bottom) collections of molecules.

Or:

5. Things, such as hammers, are collections of molecules that have significance added to them by Dasein.

Statements 3, 4, and 5 do not obviously follow from statements 1 and 2. Heidegger rejects 5. It goes against the grain of our phenomenal experience to suggest that first we perceive non-significant molecules and then superimpose value. But must ontology mirror phenomenology? Might not a hammer be *only* or *really* a collection of molecules, even if we do not usually view it in that way? It cannot be *only* a collection of molecules, as statement 3 claims. A collection of molecules that is understood or interpreted by Dasein as a hammer is not only a collection of molecules and nothing more. Dasein makes a difference. Something may not be, in a world with Dasein, precisely what it would be in a Dasein-less world. Might it be *really* or in *itself* a collection of molecules and only a hammer superficially or *for us*? But why should we say that? (As Dr Johnson said: 'Pound St Paul's church into atoms, and consider any single atom; it is, to be sure, good for nothing: but, put all these atoms together, and you have St Paul's church.') The distinction between what is so in itself and what is so only for us is a distinction drawn from our own understanding of being, not from the Dasein-independent nature of things. If there were no Dasein, there would be no such distinction: every being would be on a par with every other being, with no foreground or background, no depth and no superficiality. We do not have the resources to describe such a condition: every description we propose is already encumbered with our own understanding of being, our own significant world. Why should we say that, in our familiar Dasein-ridden world, a hammer is in *itself* a collection of molecules and only *for us* a tool? There is no reason to do so. It follows from no plausible account of a Dasein-free, hammerless world. It gives an unwarranted priority to the theoretical investigations of the scientist over the circumspect concern of the craftsman. For such reasons as these Heidegger believes that ontology and phenomenology coincide.

Chapter 7
Time, Death, and Conscience

Time played only a subdued role in Heidegger's account of Dasein's average everydayness, though it was implicit in the claim that Dasein is ahead of itself. But time, he told us in the introduction, is crucial to the question of being: 'the central problematic of all ontology is rooted in the phenomenon of time' (BT, 18). Time is also crucial for the analytic of Dasein: 'Dasein's Being finds its meaning in temporality' (BT, 19). Why is time so important?

Why Time?

Why *Being and Time*? Why not *Being and Space*? Or *Truth*? Or *Nothing*? Heidegger does not ask these questions explicitly, but he suggests a variety of answers to them. Being has traditionally been viewed in terms of time, he argues. The Greek word for being, *ousia*, is associated with the word *parousia*, which means *Anwesenheit*, 'presence' (BT, 25). So the Greeks viewed being in terms of temporal presence. This is incorrect, however. *Parousia* is only one of several compound words formed from *ousia*; there is no more reason to associate *ousia* with *parousia*-presence than with, say, *apousia*-absence. In any case, *parousia* can mean spatial presence, one's presence at a battle for example, as well as temporal presence. There may well be reason to think that the Greeks, or at least Greek philosophers, linked being with temporal presence: Plato for example ascribed being only to

6. Heidegger with Elfride at their cottage in October 1969

unchanging, eternal (or eternally *present*) forms or ideas, and not to things that 'become', arise, fade, and die away. But Heidegger has not here given us such a reason.

He notes also that philosophers have often classified entities in terms of time. They distinguish temporal entities such as men, plants, and utterances from atemporal entities such as numbers and propositions, and these again from supratemporal beings such as God (BT, 18). But this can be no more than an 'indication' that being is uniquely related to time. After all, Heidegger is ready to resist tradition, when it is appropriate to do so; he is not entitled to appeal for its support only when it suits him. In any case, he himself rejects this classification of entities. He rejects it because he does not believe that there are any atemporal or supratemporal entities. There is no supratemporal God in, above, or below Heidegger's world. If there were there might be eternal truths independent of Dasein (cf. BT, 227), but as it is the historic task of uncovering beings is performed by finite Dasein, not by God. Many philosophers in Heidegger's day, among them Husserl, postulated a 'third realm' of sense or meaning – alongside the, first realm of physical reality and the second realm of psychological reality. But this, Heidegger remarks, is 'no less questionable than medieval speculation about angels' (xxiv. 306). There are no atemporal propositions, meanings, or theories. These are all ways of Dasein's being, historical and temporal as Dasein is. The classification to which Heidegger here appeals, then, is one that he rejects.

Matters are no better if we look at the language of non-philosophers. In one of the rare passages in which Heidegger asks 'Why do we not speak just as much of being and space?' he notes that common vocabulary involves spatial more often than temporal metaphors (xxxi. 119). 'Dasein' itself is a spatial term (xx. 344). This is only natural, since Dasein is as much spatial as it is temporal, and it could not exist if it were not.

Why then is time special? One answer is that Dasein lives its life in time in a deeper sense than it lives in space. It is born in a particular place at a particular time, and neither the place nor the time is of its own choosing. *Where* I am born may of course be important, if it determines my subsequent upbringing and acculturation, whether, say, my first language is English or Japanese. But my place of birth is of little *intrinsic* importance. Even if it affects my early upbringing I can, if I wish, diminish its effects by travel and by study. But *when* I am born has effects that I cannot so readily counteract. If I am born in 1800, then I cannot read *Being and Time*, assuming that the maximum span of a human life is about 115 years. The date of my birth limits my position in time, and consequently the possible courses of action open to me, in a way that the place of my birth does not limit my position in space.

A human being needs space in which to live. A life endured in total immobility is, though conceivable, wholly unsatisfactory. But a satisfactory life need not involve extensive travel. One may live as well without ever leaving one's native town or village. But a life requires a decent time-span. Life comprises decisions and activities, and these presuppose, and take, time more crucially than space: I ask what to do now, or next, not what to do here or there.

One difference between authenticity and inauthenticity is that authentic Dasein is not wholly engrossed by the present and by the immediate past and future. Authentic Dasein looks ahead to its death and back to its birth, and beyond its birth to the historical past. Why so? Why not visit faraway places instead, if only in imagination? One answer is that spatial or geographical travel does not enable one to survey one's own life as a whole in the way that temporal or historical awareness does. Another is that my present situation and the possibilities it presents to me depend in large measure on the past, both my own past life and the past history of my culture, but hardly at all (or at least not in the same way) on what is now happening in remote places. To gain a mastery of my present situation I should read, say, Aristotle – who still influences our present way of thinking – in preference to a contemporary foreign writer who cannot have had such influence on me. Tradition is handed down over time, not across space. (This is why, when evaluating a work of art or literature, we wonder whether it will 'stand the test of time' rather than the 'test of space'.)

The life of Dasein, then, involves time more crucially than space. But Heidegger is also interested in the world and Dasein's access to it. Two traditional problems about time bear on these matters. The first is a problem that exercised Aristotle and St Augustine. Only the present moment exists now, the past no longer exists, and the future does not yet exist. So there are no temporally extended objects or events, no world enduring over time, only an instantaneous temporal slice of a world and of the objects and events within it. The second troubled

Kant and Husserl as well as the ancient thinkers. I can only perceive – see, hear, feel, and so on – what exists at the present moment – or, if we take into account the speed of light and of sound, what existed at some similarly brief past moment. So how can we ever be aware of the past or the future or a temporally enduring world? Neither of these problems concern space in the way they do time. We are not tempted to suppose that what is spatially remote from us does not exist on the ground that it does not exist *here*. Our senses, sight in particular, disclose to us a more or less extensive expanse of space from any given viewpoint.

Heidegger does not state these problems explicitly, but he was nevertheless troubled by them. His solution, a solution which is prefigured in part in Aristotle, Augustine, and Kant (BT, 427f.), is this. Dasein is not confined in its awareness to the present moment. It runs ahead into the future and reaches back into the past. Dasein is temporal. It is Dasein's temporality that makes the world genuinely temporal, that opens up 'world-time' and discloses an enduring world. Human beings are not just an insignificant biological species that developed on one of many millions of heavenly bodies, a species that has existed for only an insignificant fraction of the history of the universe. Heidegger does not reject the findings of science. Once there was no Dasein, even though there were beings. But such significance as the universe has derives from human beings. It is only this Dasein-derived significance that allows us to say that some things are significant and others trivial. The entry of Dasein into the world was an event of massive import. It was then that history, significance, worldhood, and, in a sense, time itself began. Dasein in Heidegger takes over some of the functions traditionally ascribed to God. Dasein has the advantage that it is finite, in the world, and temporal. Unlike an infinite, supratemporal, unchanging deity, Dasein is open to and opens up a world.

Heidegger does not approach time directly in the second division of BT. He begins with an account of death.

Death

Dasein, Heidegger has told us, is always ahead of itself, always poised before possibilities as yet unrealized. How then can we get a grip on Dasein as a whole? It always seems to elude our grasp, never presenting itself to us actual and complete, but always with potentialities not yet fulfilled. But there is for Dasein a final possibility, a possibility to end all possibilities, namely death.

This way of introducing death may seem far-fetched and artificial. A person cannot give a complete account of his own life even though he knows that he is going to die, since usually he does not yet know when or how he is going to die or what he is going to do in the meantime. A philosopher may give a more or less complete account of Dasein simply by saying such things as that Dasein is always ahead of itself. He does not need to specify what possibilities Dasein has or how it will actualize them. It is enough to say that it has possibilities at any moment in its career. He will of course mention death, since death is an important feature of Dasein. But the possibility of death is not a *uniquely* significant consideration in securing the completeness of the account, just one feature of Dasein among others. 'Oh, by the way,' he might say, 'I mustn't forget to add that this can't go on for ever – Dasein dies one day.'

Heidegger has, however, substantial reasons for bringing in death. First, death is not simply or even primarily something that happens at the end of one's life. Dasein's awareness that it will die, that it may die at any moment, means that 'dying', its attitude to or 'being towards' its own death, pervades, and shapes its whole life. A life without the prospect of death would be a life of perpetual postponement. Why bother to write a book now, if I have an eternity of life (and of undiminished physical and mental vigour) before me? The reason why Dasein, whether it be a philosopher or an autobiographer, cannot give a complete account of itself without death is that death haunts every moment of Dasein's life.

A second reason for introducing death is that death separates, especially sharply, the sheep from the goats, the authentic from the inauthentic. The inauthentic, lost in the anonymity of the 'they', agree that 'one dies'. This is something they chatter about, and chatter ambiguously, referring to suicide, for example, as 'doing something silly'. But they obscure the ever-present possibility, and even the imminence, of my *own* death. They treat dying as a remote possibility, as something that happens to others but not to myself – as long, that is, as I do not smoke tobacco, go to war, or 'do something silly'. The authentic person, by contrast, has a constant awareness of the possibility of his own death; he is anxious, though not fearful, in the face of it. He sees his situation and the possibilities it presents to him, and makes a decision among them, in the light of this awareness. Awareness of one's own death snatches one from the clutches of the 'they': since Dasein must die on its own – dying is not a joint or communal enterprise – death 'lays claim to it as an *individual* Dasein . . . individualizes Dasein down to itself' (BT, 263). This confers on Dasein a peculiar sort of freedom, 'freedom towards death' (BT, 266).

A third reason for introducing death is that it paves the way for Heidegger's account of time. Inauthentic and everyday Dasein are of course 'ahead of themselves' – they too have possibilities to take up – but they do not anticipate, or 'run ahead into', the possibility of death in the way that authentic Dasein does. But Dasein runs ahead only to its death, not beyond. Death will put an end to its possibilities. This means that 'original' time is *finite*, and ends with my death (BT, 330). *Time* may go on for ever, but *my* time is running out. Does this imply that I cannot reasonably insure my life so as to provide for my loved ones after my death, or arrange for the posthumous publication of my works? Surely not. It does mean that whatever arrangements I make for post-mortem effects must be made ante-mortem.

7. Heidegger at Le Thor in 1970

The 'future closes one's ability-to-be; that is the future itself is closed' (BT, 330). But the past is not closed in this way; Heidegger shows no inclination to claim that time begins with one's birth as it ends with one's death. For he is, as we shall see, vitally interested in history. But history too gives Heidegger reason to consider death. For history is made possible by death. Not in this case my own death, but the death of our ancestors. History deals with dead Dasein. Past Dasein performed glorious deeds in awareness of its own mortality and it is interestingly different from ourselves because it is dead, but not gone.

Dying

'Taken ontically', Heidegger says, 'the results of the analysis [of death] show the peculiar formality and emptiness of any ontological characterization' (BT, 248). To take the results 'ontically' is to take them as factual claims about Dasein's *Ableben*, its death or demise as a living creature. To take them 'ontologically', that is in the spirit Heidegger intends, is to take them as philosophical claims about the being of Dasein and about its *Sterben*, about Dasein's dying *as* Dasein. What are Heidegger's results? They involve the following propositions:

1. It is certain that I shall die.
2. I have to do my dying for myself. On particular occasions someone else may die in my place, as they may pay my telephone bill, or attend a meeting, on my behalf. But sooner or later I shall die in person, not by proxy.
3. That I shall die is not merely empirically likely or even empirically certain. If anyone seems not to know about death, this is really because he is 'fleeing in the face of' death (BT, 251).
4. Death will put an end to all my possibilities. I cannot do anything after I am dead.
5. It is not certain when I shall die.

6. It is possible that I shall die at any moment.

7. Dying confers wholeness on Dasein.

8. Death is 'non-relational': death severs all one's relationships to others.

Some, but not all, of these propositions look 'formal and empty'. Propositions 1 and 2 are readily acceptable, of special interest only in so far as they tend to get covered up. They do not apply uniquely to dying: if I do not die fairly soon, it is certain, for example, that I shall sleep and urinate, and that I shall do so in person. Proposition 3 is doubtful. Surely I come to know that I shall die inductively, on the basis of the previous deaths of others of my kind and also my experience of my own ageing. Heidegger agrees that 'demise' may be only 'empirically certain', but adds that this 'is in no way decisive as to the certainty of death' (BT, 257). If this is so, then 'death' must be distinct from bodily 'demise'. If the death of Dasein entailed its bodily demise, then the fact that its bodily demise is only empirically certain would entail that its death is only empirically certain. Heidegger's point is not that death and bodily demise are quite distinct events – as if a person might die as Dasein, while its body remains alive and kicking, or survive as Dasein beyond the death of its body. Death and demise are more or less simultaneous, except possibly in cases such as Nietzsche's and Hölderlin's, where bodily demise is preceded by a long period of insanity. Heidegger's idea is that my software, Dasein, is primary, and my hardware, the body, conforms to it. Thus I know non-empirically that I shall die as Dasein, but empirically that I shall die as a living organism. It does not follow that either death or demise *could* occur without the other, even if I can *imagine* one of them occurring without the other. But how can I know non-empirically that I shall die?

Proposition 4 is also questionable. I can, as we have seen, make arrangements, while alive, for what is to happen after my death. Moreover, belief in a 'life after death' has been, and perhaps still is, quite widespread. Heidegger claims that his 'ontological' account leaves this possibility open:

> If 'death' is defined as the 'end' of Dasein – that is to say, of Being-in-the-world – this does not imply any ontical decision whether 'after death' still another Being is possible, either higher or lower, or whether Dasein 'lives on' or even 'outlasts' itself and is 'immortal'.
>
> (BT, 247f.)

Heidegger claims that his account might be accepted by anyone, whether or not they believe in immortality, and that this issue can be properly discussed only after we have given such a non-committal account of death. But is his account really compatible with immortality? If Dasein is essentially in the world, how could it survive as Dasein once it is no longer in the world? If it does not survive as Dasein, what else might it survive as? Or might Dasein after death somehow continue to be in a world, retaining a ghostly presence in this world, or passing into another world? Heidegger barely allows a place for beliefs such as these. Yet implausible as they are, they are not so obviously absurd that denial of them is 'formal and empty'.

Proposition 5 is true enough. Even if I have resolved to kill myself at a definite time, it is not certain that I shall live until then, that I shall carry out my resolve, or that the bomb will go off on time. Proposition 6 seems to follow from 5, but in fact it does not. It is, for example, not possible that I shall die in 200 years' time, though this is because it is certain that I shall die within the next 100 years; it is uncertain when I shall die only within limits. But the main problem with proposition 6 lies not in what it says but in what it does *not* say. Though it is *possible* that I shall die at, or before, 10 o'clock this evening, it is very *unlikely*. The way in which I order my life depends no doubt on my certainty that I shall die at some time and my uncertainty when I shall die. I would not be writing this book now, if I knew that I would live for ever, or if I knew that I was going to die at 10 o'clock tonight. But equally I would not do so (or at least I would not sign a contract to do so) if I did not think it fairly likely that I would live to complete it. Why does Heidegger neglect probability, when it is as important for the management of my life as possibility? Partly because he associates probability with statistics concerning the longevity of man as a biological species (BT, 246). They deal with demise rather than death. And even if the statistics concern people of my type – middle-aged English male sedentary pipe-smoking academics – they do not concern my death in particular, but the deaths of people of my *type*. But it is hard to see how a reasonable ordering of one's life could dispense with some estimate of one's life expectancy, whether it be based on informal observation of the fate of relevantly similar others or on how one 'feels in oneself'.

A second reason why Heidegger neglects probability is that Dasein is its possibility, Dasein can decide how to be. Does this mean that at any moment I can kill myself? This seems unlikely. First, it is not true that one can kill oneself at any moment, even if it is possible for one to die at that moment. He quotes with approval an old saying: 'As soon as a man comes to life, he is at once old enough to die.' True enough. One can die in infancy. But one cannot usually kill oneself in infancy. Nor can one do so if one is asleep, hopelessly drunk, or bound in chains. Again, Heidegger disapproves of suicide as a response to the possibility of death, since it converts the possibility into an actuality instead of letting it remain a possibility (xx. 439). The very inadequacy of this argument against suicide suggests that he has a deeply rooted prejudice against it and that he does not have it in mind when he speaks of the constant possibility of death. If death is a possibility, but not a possibility that is, in the usual sense, to be chosen, why can we not speak of death at a given moment or within a given period as probable or as unlikely?

Proposition 7 supplies Heidegger's best argument for the view that

Dasein knows non-empirically that it will die. Dasein is care; it has to order its life by undertaking various projects and allowing a certain time for them. How could it do that if it had an eternity of time at its disposal? It could not, any more than I could be a prudent financial manager if I had an infinite amount of wealth at my disposal. But a prudent manager of life or finances needs to know more than Heidegger allows. He needs to know not just that his life will end or his resources are limited. He needs to know roughly how long he can expect to live, or how much wealth he has. I cannot manage my funds wisely if I do not know whether I have £10 billion or £100. I cannot manage my life prudently if I have no idea whether I shall live for one minute or 500 years. If in the natural course of events people matured at around 20 years of age and then had 500 years of active life ahead of them, they might be more averse to risk, less ready to sacrifice their remaining centuries in wars or on mountain peaks than we are to forgo the years or decades left to us.

Heidegger does not allow Dasein enough knowledge to exist as care. But what it requires to exist as care need not be *knowledge*. If I believe that I have about £100,000 available, I may manage my funds prudently – even if in fact and unbeknown to myself I have £10 billion or even an infinity of wealth. Likewise, Dasein may exist as care if it *thinks* it will die at around 75, even if it will in fact live far longer or even forever. Unlike the prudent fund manager, Dasein is bound to realize sooner or later that it has far more years available than it originally supposed (unless it is subject to periodic memory loss), though it need never establish that it is immortal. What matters for care is not so much that Dasein *will* die, but that it *believes* that it will die. Heidegger need not disagree with this: the important thing for him is 'dying', one's being towards death, not dying or death in the ordinary senses.

United in Death?

Proposition 8 is connected with propositions 2 and 4. If death puts an end to all my possibilities (4), then I cannot, after my death, be actively related to other people (8); I may be loved or remembered by others, but I cannot love or remember them in return. If I have to die in person, not just by proxy (2), then again I cannot be related, in my death or my dying, to other people by the relation of proxyship or representation. But there is more to proposition 8 than that. Dying is not like loving, where someone is the object of the love even if the love is unrequited. It is not like playing chess, which (usually) requires two people to play together. It is more like solitaire. Even when two or more people die together, they are like people playing solitaire in the same room. Or like two people sleeping together (in the literal sense) in the same bed. Everyone, we might say, dies alone. And we can add: everyone sleeps alone.

Usually dying is a solitary business. But must it be so? Why cannot dying, the process of dying, be more like chess or dancing, where what each person does depends on what the other does? We arrange to shoot each other at the same time. Two lovers die of grief, since each believes the other to be dying. Warriors stay to die holding the pass, but each does so only on condition that the others do. Much as lovers fall asleep in each other's arms, each doing so when and because the other does so.

The process of dying, however, terminates in death, the state of being dead. In death one cannot be related to others as one may be in dying. Death is not unique in this respect. In dreamless sleep one cannot be related to others as one may be in falling asleep. Only we usually wake up from sleep and renew our relations to others. But why, even so, need death 'individualize Dasein down to itself'? There are two reasons for doubting that it must. First, though one is not, in death, related to others, nor is one a lone individual, immured in solitary confinement.

In death, one is not related to others, but not isolated from them either; one simply *is not*. Second, although a dead person cannot *from his own point of view* be related to others – since he no longer has a point of view – it may seem to him before his death, and to others after his death, that he has important relations to others in *death*. The Athenians who fell at Marathon, and the Spartans who fell at Thermopylae, were buried together in common graves; it seemed important to their contemporaries that this should be so, to mark their comradeship in death as well as in dying. Nowadays appropriate burial is supposed to require an individual grave, but people often wish to be buried near to definite others. Heidegger himself wanted to lie beside his parents in Messkirch. When he expressed this wish, the prospect of his death did not individualize him down to his bare self; he was the son of Friedrich and Johanna Heidegger, a native of Messkirch, united in death to his fellow townsmen. Was that inauthentic? No more so, surely, than his concern for the posthumous publication of his works. But at least, Heidegger might reply, taking seriously the prospect of your own death forces you to consider what relations to which others importantly matter to *yourself*. You can no longer remain dispersed in the inauthenticity of the *they*, content to be buried with your family (or with your fallen comrades) simply because that is what 'one' does. Can I not? Is it less reasonable to submit to custom in the disposal of my corpse than in the choice of my clothes? Still, Heidegger believed, at this stage of his career at least, that dying individualizes Dasein: 'In a way, it is only in dying that I can say absolutely "I am"' (xx. 440).

Authentic Dasein runs ahead to its own death. How does it do that? The answer lies in conscience.

Conscience

The problem is this. If Dasein runs ahead to its own death, then it can escape the clutches of the 'they' and make an authentic choice about its own way of being, not simply accept the limited range of possibilities allowed it by 'them'. But how can it do that? 'They' already cater for death. *They* tell me not to worry about it, it's a remote possibility. So Dasein remains in the embrace of the 'they'. In this condition Dasein does not really have a conscience, it is not responsible for what it is and does, and it is not guilty of anything. 'They' take responsibility for things, since all I am and do I am and do because it is what 'one' is and does. Guilt and responsibility are placed on 'their' shoulders. I do not even make real choices: I just follow the routines that 'they' prescribe.

Conscience in the traditional sense commands or forbids certain actions on moral grounds. Often it is regarded as a voice that calls to one, sometimes, though not invariably, the voice of God. In this sense of 'conscience', someone mired in the they-self lacks a conscience. Conscience tells *me* what to do and what not to do, me as an individual self, not the they-self. It may tell me not to do what *they* do, or to do what they do not do. If I have not yet eluded the they-self, I cannot have a conscience in this sense: I do not view myself as an individual distinct from others, making choices on his own account. Heidegger uses the same word, *Gewissen*, both for conscience in this traditional sense and for conscience in his own more fundamental sense, but it will be convenient to distinguish them as, respectively, 'conscience' and 'Conscience'. Not everyone has a traditional conscience, but everyone has a Conscience. A Conscience tells me not what specific choices to make or avoid, what actions to take or omit, but calls on me to make a choice, to take action, and to bear my own responsibility for it. Before I can choose, I have to choose to choose, and it is to this choice that Conscience calls me. Only when I have chosen choice, answered the call of Conscience, can I have a conscience. If I hear the call of Conscience, it is because I want to have a Conscience. Everyone has a Conscience and it calls to them continuously. But not everyone responds to it, and no one responds all the time. That is why the call of conscience is only intermittent.

If I am wholly in thrall to the 'they', how can I ever hear the call of Conscience? How can there be a call of Conscience? The call does not come from God, nor from any third party. This would not help to answer our question. We could still ask: Why do some hear God's call and others not? Does he call louder to some and more softly to others? Or are some heavier sleepers than others? Then the call of Conscience would be like an alarm-clock ringing just loud enough to wake light sleepers. But the call does not come from outside. It comes from Dasein itself; Dasein calls to Dasein. It can come from Dasein itself, because Dasein is never wholly and irretrievably lost in the *they*. Dasein retreats into the security of the *they* owing to a 'fleeing of Dasein in the face of itself – of itself as an authentic ability to be it Self' (BT, 184). But Dasein must have a glimpse of that from which it flees. It is this residual awareness of its authentic self that enables Dasein both to call to itself and on occasion to respond to the call.

Guilt and Nullity

When Dasein responds to the call of Conscience, does it want to have a conscience as well as a Conscience? Does it acquire a conscience in the traditional sense? Heidegger does not seem to answer these questions in the affirmative. The call of Conscience, like that of conscience, reveals to Dasein that it is *guilty*. But Guilt in this sense (again the initial capital 'G' marks Heidegger's special use of the word) is not something to which Dasein succumbs only occasionally. Every Dasein is Guilty, but only authentic Dasein realizes its Guilt and acts in full awareness of it. The idea of a primordial, ineradicable Guilt is not original to Heidegger. He sometimes ascribes it to Goethe: 'The agent is, as Goethe also said, always unscrupulous [*gewissenlos*, lit. 'conscienceless']. I can only be really unscrupulous, when I have chosen wanting-to-have-a-conscience' (xx. 441). It is only because everyone is Guilty that anyone can be guilty.

Why is Dasein Guilty? There are several ideas in play. Dasein makes a choice *itself*; it cannot unload the responsibility for it onto *them* or onto someone else. Dasein chooses one possibility from among several; it inevitably neglects some worthwhile possibilities in favour of the one it has chosen. Any choice will have consequences that Dasein did not foresee or intend, but for these too it must take responsibility. An authentic choice is likely to offend against the rules established by *them*. Above all, when Dasein makes its choice, choosing for itself a way of being not for the next two days but for its whole life, it has no ultimate reason for making this choice rather than an alternative: 'we define the formal existential idea of the "Guilty" as: Being-the-basis for a Being which has been defined by a "not" that is, as Being-the-basis of a nullity' (BT, 283).

Why is Dasein the basis of a nullity? In its average everydayness, the decisions Dasein takes follow naturally from what it has done earlier. I have promised, say, to have Martin's shoes ready by tomorrow, so I should get to work on them this afternoon. Even if I face a dilemma – Should I allow Martin credit, and if so, how much? – there are fairly well-established procedures for resolving it. *They* know what I should do in such situations; I can always do what they say I should. But it is different if I am choosing the course of my life as a whole. Shall I remain a shoemaker or shall I become a missionary or enter politics? Nothing in my past life naturally favours one of these options over the others, since I am deciding not what step to take next within an already predetermined life-plan, but how my life should go as a whole. Nor is it any use consulting *them*. They will very likely say it would be silly to give up making shoes. But in any case what they say is no longer relevant. I am choosing my own life, not theirs, and the fact that I am doing so implies that I have broken free of their grip. Running ahead to my death and turning back to my birth has taken the place of appeal to the they-self as a way of deciding matters. But then my choice seems to lack any basis outside itself. The life I project for myself is a nullity. Matters look no better if I reflect on the range of options open to me. This is no longer a menu presented to me by *them*, it is true. But it is restricted by a situation that I did not myself choose. I cannot for example become a knight in armour or an astronaut. In contrast to the everyday view of things, the life-choice to which Conscience calls me seems thoroughly contingent. As Dr Johnson said: 'To prefer one future mode of life to another, upon just reasons, requires faculties which it has not pleased our Creator to give us.'

Resoluteness

What then does authentic Dasein do? It becomes resolute, *entschlossen*, a word which is related to *erschlossen*, 'disclosed', and itself means literally 'dis-, un-closed'. Thus: 'Resoluteness [*Entschlossenheit*] is a distinctive mode of Dasein's disclosedness [*Erschlossenheit*]' (BT, 297). Resoluteness discloses Dasein itself in a new way; Dasein surveys its life as a whole from its birth to its death. It discloses the world and things in it, including other people, in a new way. It thus discloses a range of possibilities that are not visible to everyday Dasein, lost in the they. Heidegger's account of resoluteness is coloured by his study of the conversions of St Paul, St Augustine, and Martin Luther. Paul is in the same world after seeing the light on the road to Damascus as he was before, but everything looks different. Resoluteness confers on Dasein's decisions a fateful necessity despite the nullity of its projection: Luther says not 'Perhaps this is what I should do', but 'Here I stand; I cannot do otherwise.' In resoluteness Dasein pulls itself together as well as opens itself up. Later in BT Heidegger uses the term *Augenblick* – literally 'eye-glance', but the ordinary German for 'instant' or 'moment' – for the 'moment of vision' in which resolute Dasein assesses the possibilities implicit in its situation and makes a decisive choice.

What choice should resolute Dasein make? Can its choice be right or wrong? Are there any criteria for telling whether it is right or wrong? Conscience in the traditional sense is often held to be open to error. Can resoluteness err? Heidegger gives no indication that it can, or that there is any way in which a choice might be assessed apart from the resoluteness in which it is made. After all, authentic Dasein cannot simply follow what they say about right and wrong, nor can it appeal to any established moral code. Any code or criterion that might be suggested to it is itself something that has to be chosen or rejected.

Karl Löwith records a joke devised by one of Heidegger's students: 'I am resolved, only towards what I don't know' (Löwith, 30). This is unfair. A resolute person knows very well what he has to do, even if it is only that he, like Paul, must wait for God's command. But there is no single thing that every resolute person has to do, nor are there any rules by which we, or a given person, can decide what he has to do. Heidegger himself was resolute in the pursuit of philosophy, but this is not something that he could recommend to everyone or even to those who are equipped for it. Heidegger always declined to write a work on ethics. A 'concrete moral code', he implies, does not depend on our possession of an 'ethic as an absolutely binding science' (xvii. 85). We all know, without the help of philosophy or ethics that we should, in normal circumstances, pay our debts and keep our promises. But when it comes to momentous choices about the conduct of our lives, a concrete moral code is of little help. Either it gives no unequivocal answer to our problem or it is itself open to question. But an 'ethic as an absolutely binding science' would be no use either. It too leaves the matter undecided or is open to question. Heidegger's attitude to fundamental choices is similar to his view of truth. There is no truth in the sense of correspondence to the facts nor are there, in the most fundamental cases, any criteria for telling whether a view is true or not. The best one can do is to be 'primordial', to go back as far as one can towards the source, disregarding the current wisdom of the they. So it is with choice. There are no objectively correct answers to life's basic problems nor any decision procedure for discerning them. The best one can do is to be resolute, to withdraw from the crowd, and to make one's decision in view of one's life as a whole. One's choices, like one's assertions, are always made in a specific situation. What looks good to me in this situation may not look so good to others now or later, or even to myself in a later situation. But there is no remedy for that. The only guarantee that what I do now, writing this book for example, will meet with my approval twenty years hence is to postpone it for twenty years.

Why be Resolute?

One Dasein heeds the call of Conscience and in resolute authenticity runs ahead to its death. Another Dasein does not. Is the former better than the latter? If so, why? Why is it better to be resolute than to drift with the tide of everydayness? If Heidegger were recommending resoluteness, he would be proposing a sort of ethic. Not, it is true, a very definite ethic as far as our conduct is concerned. Resolute Dasein need not decide to abandon shoemaking in favour of some more exhilarating mode of life. But if it does continue making shoes, it does so 'with the sober anxiety which brings us face to face with our individualized ability to be, . . . an unshakable joy in this possibility' (BT, 310). This, he implies, is better than making shoes simply because it never occurs to you to do anything else.

Resoluteness is not *morally* better than irresoluteness. It does not guarantee or even make it more likely that we shall behave in a morally better way. (Hitler was no less resolute than Christ or Socrates.) Nor is resoluteness intrinsically morally superior to irresoluteness. The advantage of resoluteness is that resolute Dasein discloses itself, its possibilities, and its wholeness, in a way that irresolute Dasein does not. Everyday fallen Dasein tends, as we have seen, to misinterpret itself: 'the entity which we ourselves are, is ontologically that which is farthest' (BT, 311; cf. BT, 15). (Cf. lxiii. 32: 'Dasein speaks of itself, it sees itself in a certain way, and yet it is only a mask, which it holds before itself so that it does not terrify itself.') We need to look at resolute Dasein to see what Dasein is really like. But this begs several questions. Does Heidegger suppose that resolute Dasein is *really* Dasein in a way that irresolute Dasein is not? If so, with what right? Most of us for most of the time are irresolute. Why assume that we come into our own only when we are resolute? Or that only resolute Dasein sees itself as it really is? If irresolute Dasein interprets itself as a thing among other things or as one of the crowd, why assume that it is wrong to do so? Resolute Dasein may not be a *thing*, but perhaps irresolute Dasein is.

Heidegger's reply is this. Both resoluteness and irresoluteness, both authenticity and inauthenticity, are ways of Dasein's being. In this respect neither has priority over the other. But irresolute, inauthentic Dasein cannot give an adequate interpretation of its own condition or of resoluteness. In a similar way when one is asleep or day-dreaming one cannot give an adequate account *either* of sleep and day-dreaming *or* of wakefulness and alertness. To interpret everydayness or dispersal in the 'they' requires a withdrawal from, or elevation above, these states. Throughout his life, Heidegger was influenced by Plato's allegory in the *Republic*: ordinary men are prisoners in a cave, looking at shadows on the wall; some of them escape into the world above, where they see real objects and eventually the sun itself; they return into the cave to persuade the other prisoners to escape. Only one who has escaped from the cave can give a proper account of the condition in the cave, as well as of what is outside the cave. Similarly only the resolute can give an account of irresolution or of resoluteness. To be a philosopher one must be resolute. One must, first, withdraw from the round of everydayness. And secondly, one must rise above the current philosophical situation and the tradition that lies behind it. One cannot, if one wants to do more than humdrum routine philosophy, simply absorb the concepts, doctrines, and problems handed down by the philosophical tradition. One has to run ahead to one's own death and return to the past, back to the source of the philosophical tradition. Then one masters the tradition and is not mastered by it. And one has left *them* far behind. Or as Heidegger puts it: 'the research which wants to develop and conceptualize that kind of Being which belongs to existence, is itself a kind of Being which disclosive Dasein possesses; can such research be denied this projecting which is essential to Dasein?' (BT, 315). No more, surely, than Dasein can be expected to philosophize in its sleep.

Chapter 8
Temporality, Transcendence, and Freedom

Time has now come into its own. Dasein can only be resolute in time or over time. But we should not say that Dasein is 'in' time or 'over' time. Time is not like a container that Dasein is in, any more than the world is. In fact what is primary is not time (*Zeit*), but Dasein's timeliness or temporality (*Zeitlichkeit*). This is a standard move in Heidegger: the primary phenomenon is not the world, space, time, or history, but Dasein's being in the world, Dasein's spatiality, Dasein's temporality, or Dasein's historicity. What at first looks like a thing or substance, denoted by a noun, becomes a way of Dasein's being, denoted by an adjective or adverb. Dasein is placed at the centre of things. 'Time is Dasein' (CT, 20). Not only that. Time is my time, the time of an individual Dasein: 'In so far as time is in each case mine, there are many times. Time itself is meaningless; time is temporal' (CT, 21). It sounds as if time is hopelessly subjective – if it were not for Heidegger's insistence that Dasein is not a 'subject' – as if each resolute agent has its own time, ending with its own death and unrelated to the time of any other agent. But matters are not as bad as that. Intersubjective 'world-time', *the* time that is the same for all Dasein, is restored – as a derivative phenomenon, but none the less real.

There are in BT at least four notions of time or temporality. First, 'primordial' or 'authentic' temporality, the temporality of resolute Dasein. Second, inauthentic temporality, the temporality of everyday and/or fallen Dasein. Thirdly, world-time, the public time in which we encounter beings within the world. Finally, 'vulgar' or 'ordinary' time, time as conceived by philosophers from Aristotle to Bergson, time as a homogeneous, unending sequence of 'nows' or instants. Each of these notions of time (except the first) derives, on Heidegger's view, from the preceding. This too is a regular feature of his procedure. He does not begin (as Husserl might do) from the apparently simpler phenomenon – time as a sequence of instants, or, in other cases, living organisms or the merely present at hand – and then construct the more complex phenomenon – authentic temporality, Dasein, or the ready to hand – on this basis. He begins with the richer, more complex phenomenon and derives the simpler phenomenon from it by successively 'modifying' it and, in some cases, by stripping away some of its features. Non-human animals, for example, are to be understood 'privatively', as creatures that lack certain features that Dasein has; Dasein is not to be seen as an animal with something else, reason say, added to it. Heidegger proceeds in this way, from the complex to the simple, for reasons both of phenomenology and of ontology. We do not naturally view ourselves as animal organisms with reason superimposed on them, or the time of our decision as a sequence of homogeneous instants with significance conferred upon it by our resolution. The complex is not *composite*: it is not built up by the combination of simpler elements, and it cannot be analysed as if it were. Historically, time, or at least our experience of time, did not first enter the world as a tedious now-sequence; it first arose as the time of resolute Dasein, Dasein striving to impose order and significance on an apparently hostile or indifferent environment.

Authentic Temporality

Resolute Dasein runs ahead to its death, and reaches back into the past, before deciding what to do in the present, the authentic present or *Augenblick*, the moment of vision. It goes back to the past, since it cannot fully grasp its present situation or decide how to act in it unless it knows how it reached its present situation. I cannot, for example, decide how to continue writing from this point unless I know something about what I have written earlier in this book. This is so, even if the continuation is relatively unproblematic. I shall need to explore my earlier writing, and perhaps beyond, more seriously if my decision is more problematic, if, say, I have decided to restructure the book entirely or I have got into a muddle owing to some false assumption that I have been making all along. Resolute Dasein, however, goes back further than that. How far and where to? Back to Messkirch in 1889? Or back to Plato in the fourth century BCE? Heidegger occasionally mentions birth: 'Dasein exists as born; and, as born, it is already dying, in the sense of Being-towards-death. As long as Dasein factically exists, both the "ends" and their "between" *are*' (BT, 374). But he does not mention it nearly as often as death; nor does he suggest that time begins with one's birth as it ends with one's death. And this is reasonable. One's active life begins with one's birth as it ends with one's death. But the past time that bears on one's present situation need not begin with one's birth. In some decisions one reverts to one's birth. In deciding to be buried in Messkirch Heidegger needed to recall that he was born there. But other decisions invoke a larger span of the past. In deciding to reconsider the question of being he needed to return to the philosophers of ancient Greece, not simply to the philosophy written after his birth. Of course anything one does or produces can be considered *both* in the context of one's own life *and* in the larger context of a historical tradition. Heidegger's marriage or his burial belong to a tradition of marriages and of burials as well as to his own life. *Being and Time* too can be seen as an event in Heidegger's life as well as a stage in the philosophical tradition that began in the seventh century BCE. It seems appropriate, when deciding on marriage or burial, to focus on one's own life and simply take the tradition for granted. But it would not be natural to do this when deciding how to write a work such as *Being and Time*. One's own life is relevant to the decision *whether* to write a book at all. But once one has decided to write a philosophy book, one's own life (including, say, one's prospects of gaining tenure) recedes into the background, and the philosophical tradition comes into sharper focus. In running ahead into the future, by contrast, I cannot go beyond, at least not much beyond, my own death. Quite likely philosophy, as well as other things, will continue after my death, but my idea of what it will be like is too hazy for me to take much account of it. At most I can arrange for the posthumous publication of my works, in the hope that they will be read, understood, and believed.

Resolute Dasein, then, has a future that ends with its death, a past that extends back to its birth and perhaps beyond, and a present. Heidegger calls these 'ecstases', from a Greek word meaning literally 'standing outside, forth', hence 'removal, displacement', and, later, 'being beside oneself, or out of one's mind, in an ecstatic mental state'. ('Ecstasis' is related to 'existence' and has the same root meaning.) Temporality, Heidegger argues, essentially involves these ecstases. They figure either not at all, or only as later additions, in the conception of time as a series of instants. What matters to Galileo as a physicist is *how long* two balls of different weights take to roll down a slope, not whether they do so in the past, present, or future. But Galileo had to decide to perform this experiment, and this decision involved the ecstatic temporality of resolute Dasein, with a past, a present, and a future.

The future is the primary ecstasis, certainly for resolute Dasein, but also, with 'modification', for irresolute Dasein. Time is essentially and primarily time for doing something, time to do something, and this involves the future more immediately than the past or the present. The German for 'future' is *Zukunft*, literally 'to-coming, coming to(wards)'; the root idea is that events come to us, or approach, out of the future. Heidegger gives a different interpretation: Dasein runs ahead to its own death and then 'comes towards itself' out of the future. It does not return simply to the present. It recoils from the future, from its own death, back into the past. The ordinary German for the 'past' is

Vergangenheit. But this suggests to Heidegger the past as dead and gone. The past to which Dasein rebounds is the past that lives on in the present, the past that informs its present situation and the possibilities inherent in it. For this he uses *Gewesenheit*, 'having-been-ness'. Dasein's past is not something dead and gone that it has left behind. The relevant past, the past that bears on its present situation, emerges from the future. Dasein then rebounds from the past into the present and it is there that it decides on action. The ordinary German for the 'present' is *Gegenwart*, literally 'waiting towards', but Heidegger gives it an active flavour by associating it with a verb, *gegenwärtigen*, to 'make present': 'Only as the Present in the sense of making present, can resoluteness be what it is: namely, letting itself be encountered undisguisedly by that which it seizes upon in taking action' (BT, 326). 'Making present' is to the present what 'retaining' is to the past and 'waiting' or expecting is to the future; Heidegger avoids anything so specific and detached as 'perceiving'. Irresolute, as well as resolute, Dasein has a *Gegenwart*. Only resolute Dasein has an *Augenblick*, a moment of vision.

Temporality and Care

Dasein's ability at any moment to traverse its whole life – to run ahead to its death, return to its birth, and rebound into the present – is what makes it a unified self: Dasein bursts asunder into past, present, and future and then pulls itself together again – more like a piece, of elastic than beads on a string. The triadic structure of temporality corresponds to various other triads that we have come across in our earlier account of Dasein. Heidegger thus 'repeats' or reworks the earlier results in view of their temporality. Care has, as we have seen, a threefold structure: it is '[1] ahead-of-itself-[2] Being-already-in-(the-world) as [3] Being-alongside (entities encountered within-the-world)' (BT, 192). The first element, being ahead of oneself, involves primarily the future. Every Dasein is ahead of itself, is up to something. In resoluteness this takes the form of running ahead to death, while in inauthenticity it is diluted to a mere 'awaiting', waiting to see what will happen and being ready to deal with it. The future also corresponds to understanding, which is essentially directed to the future: it is knowing how to cope with things and, in its most authentic form, knowing how to live. With the future too belongs existence, Dasein's supervision of its own being. The second element of care, being already in the world, involves the past. Dasein has been 'thrown' into the world, it is encumbered with 'facticity', contingent features of itself and of its situation that are not its doing and that it simply has to make the most of. Thrownness and facticity are disclosed by moods such as anxiety, which are primarily directed to the past. (Anxiety is past-directed, since it is 'anxious about naked Dasein as something that has been thrown into uncanniness' (BT, 343). Anxiety's inauthentic counterpart, fear, is also past-directed, since it involves having 'forgotten oneself' in one's bewilderment (BT, 342).) The third element, being alongside entities encountered within the world, primarily involves the present, 'making present', in the sense of 'letting oneself be encountered by', things in one's current situation. Falling too pertains to the present: fallen Dasein concerns itself with what is present, its immediate business or the current gossip, rather than with the long-term past or future. Talk or discourse, which ranks alongside understanding, mood, and falling as a central feature of Dasein, does not belong to any ecstasis, but ranges over all three of them; tenses are essential to discourse.

Temporality and Being-in-the-World

Everyday Dasein is mostly irresolute. This need not mean that it is fickle and vacillating, that it does not do its job. It has its job to do and it concentrates on that, without bothering whether this is a fitting way to spend its life. It is in a way absorbed in the present rather than the future. It is wielding a tool, a hammer say, to bang a nail in leather. But 'one tool', Heidegger insists, 'is ontologically impossible' (BT, 353). A tool is always part of an implicit network of interreferential equipment in the workplace. (The 'impossibility' is only 'ontological': Heidegger does not exclude the 'ontical' possibility of my having only one tool because the others have been stolen or lost in a shipwreck. He does exclude the possibility that I have invented a wheel but have not yet thought of anything to do with it.) When I am using the hammer, I make it present. It is what I am focusing on at present. How then is the workshop as a whole *there* for me? It could not be, if I did no more than make things present. I do not at present have the whole workshop in my sights, still less do I see or explicitly think about my customers. I 'retain' the equipment that I am not presently using, my customers, and so on. I do not explicitly recall them, I have a muted awareness of their presence. I have in a way forgotten them too, just as I have forgotten myself in my absorption in my task. This is the everyday relationship to the past. Similarly I 'await' or expect certain things – in a subdued sense quite distinct from that in which I expect my horse to win. I expect my hammer to function properly, I expect my nails to be there when I want another, I do not expect to touch a rat as I reach for a nail. I notice broken tools, missing tools, and unexpected intruders. I could not do this, if 'concernful dealings were merely a sequence of "experiences" running their course "in time"'. All this must 'be grounded in the ecstatical unity of the making-present which awaits and retains' (BT, 355). So it is time that makes possible being-in-the-world, time as ecstatic temporality.

Time, Transcendence, and Freedom

Occasionally in BT (364ff.), but more often in later works (xxvi; ER), Heidegger identifies being-in-the-world with Dasein's 'transcendence'. Dasein transcends, not in the sense that it either is or attains to some other-worldly entity, nor in the sense that it manages to get over the barriers of its own subjectivity and make contact with an external object – there are no such barriers. Dasein transcends, steps beyond, any and every particular entity to the world in which they lie. What if Dasein did not transcend? Stones do not transcend, nor do insects, dogs, or God. Stones, insects, and dogs are in varying degrees crowded in by the things in their environment. Everything they do is determined by their immediate surroundings. Things are too close, too oppressive, to be 'encountered'. God too cannot encounter entities, not because they crowd him in, but because they are wholly his creation, wholly and eternally transparent to him and at his beck and call. Dasein by contrast transcends other entities and projects a world in which they lie at a critical distance from Dasein itself. Thus Dasein is (unlike God) finite, in the midst of beings which it allows to be themselves, and thus encounters rather than creates. But (unlike stones or animals) Dasein has free space in which to live, beyond the control of its immediate environment or of any given entity. Dasein leaves things alone and they leave it alone.

Take an analogy: In a self-enclosed hierarchical group (a patriarchal family, say) the members cannot choose their relationships – to whom and how they relate. Those at the bottom of the hierarchy are at the bidding of those above them; their every relationship and much of their conduct is moulded by their superiors. These are the insects. The person at the top of the hierarchy has all those below him in his control; what they do is determined by him. He is God. Neither the insects nor God encounter genuine *others*, only immovable oppressors or pliable vassals. But Dasein transcends every such other and every such relationship. It does not have to associate with this person or that, in this way or that. It can choose its 'being-with', how and with whom it associates. It can let the others be as they are, independent others who are not at its beck and call as it is not at theirs. This does not mean that Dasein can do as it likes. Others place constraints on it. Dasein is not God. So it is with Dasein's being-in-the-world. Dasein allows free play to other beings, including other Dasein, and they leave it free space. Only then can it encounter other beings. It does not first encounter other beings, and then superimpose worldhood and significance on them. It cannot encounter them at all unless it transcends them to a world and then returns from it to particular entities, as a spider spins a web and encounters flies within it. (Dasein steers a path too between realism and idealism. If realism, or materialism, were right Dasein would be like an insect. If idealism were right, he would be like God. But Dasein is in between: between God and insects, between birth and death, and between itself and the world.)

Dasein's transcendence depends on its ecstatic temporality in a way that no other entity has, Dasein has a future, a past, and a present. Each of these ecstases is a 'horizon' or rather a field bounded by a horizon. Each is defined by one of three aspects of purposive human activity, and this is its 'horizonal schema' or 'pattern'. First, the 'for the sake of itself', that is, Dasein's aims and purposes – the schema of the future. (Dasein is not essentially *egotistical*. My aim may be to help others, but it is nevertheless *my* aim.) Second, that 'in the face of which' Dasein is thrown, the background situation which is not of my own making – the schema of the past. Finally, the 'in order to', the equipment I use to achieve my purposes and aims – the schema of the present.

Ecstatic temporality transcends particular entities in two respects. First, an ecstasis is not simply the aggregate of things and events encountered in it. I run ahead into the future knowing little about what will happen in the future, apart from my own chronologically indeterminate death. When I return to the past, I do not retrace every past event in reverse chronological order until I reach, say, my birth. I have forgotten most of these events, even if I once experienced them, so I return without more ado to the relevantly significant past. Secondly, ecstatic temporality treats particular entities primarily as possibilities rather than actualities. The past into which I am thrown is significant not for what it starkly is, but for the possibilities it presents for continuing my life. The hammer on the bench is not just something actual. It is something I may or may not use, something I may use for this purpose or for that, beyond the hammer itself and my use of it.

Dasein transcends its own present state. The interest of my present state lies in what it enables me to do or become.

So Dasein transcends to world and Dasein transcends in temporality. These ways of transcending look similar in structure. But why should we agree with Heidegger that they are essentially connected, that Dasein transcends temporally if, and only if, it transcends to world, let alone that its worldly transcendence is based on its temporal transcendence? No doubt there could be no world, in Heidegger's sense, without temporality. But might there not be temporality without a world? There could not, for at least two reasons. First, there cannot be temporality without entities, other entities, that is, than Dasein itself. Time is not just a series of nows. It is time for doing things with things. Time is dated by reference to things and events, the time of my birth, for example, or the time of so-and-so's death. Moreover, things and events cannot simply be strung out along time without belonging, even at a single time, to a world. The nails I shall need later are even now in a box in the cupboard. The town of Messkirch, where I was once born and where one day I shall be buried, is there even now, though I have not been there for some time. Time spills over into the world. Secondly, Dasein's freedom, which is secured by its temporality, requires, as we have seen, being-in-a-world. Given that there are beings, Dasein must transcend them, place them in a world, and keep them at a distance.

Is Dasein really free? Are its choices and actions not caused by, or grounded in, other things and events out of its control? Not on Heidegger's view. In later works he argues that grounds presuppose Dasein's freedom rather than eradicate it (xxvi; xxxi; ER). If entities were regarded as simply actual, we would not ask after their grounds. We only ask for the ground or cause of something, the French Revolution, say, or Stonehenge, if we regard it as possibly otherwise, as only one possibility among others. But it is Dasein's freedom and transcendence that enables, indeed requires, it to view entities as possibilities rather than sheer actualities. Hence Dasein asks for the grounds of things. It asks 'why?': 'Man is not primarily the no-sayer . . ., nor is he the yes-sayer; he is the why-asker' (xxvi. 280). Dasein regards any particular being as a possibility and asks for its ground. It can also ask for the ground of all beings together. It can ask: 'Why is there anything at all rather than nothing?' (xxvi; IM). It asks this, because in its resolute, anxious moments, it views the whole of beings as a possibility rather than a sheer actuality. Thus not only empirical science, but metaphysics – philosophy in the grand manner of Leibniz and Schelling – is deeply rooted in Dasein's freedom: 'metaphysics belongs to the nature of man . . . to exist is already to philosophize' (xxvi. 274).

Heidegger takes seriously Kant's doctrine of the primacy of practical reason – more seriously, perhaps, than Kant did.

Chapter 9
History and World-Time

Heidegger interrupts his account of time in BT to consider, in chapter 5 of Division II, 'Temporality and Historicality'. His interest in history dates back to 1916, when in an article on 'The Concept of Time in the Study of History' he argued that the historian cannot regard time, as the natural scientist does, as purely quantitative and uniform. Historical time involves qualitatively distinct periods, such as the Victorian era, whose significance depends on more than their length as measured in years. History had become a thriving discipline in nineteenth-century Germany, and philosophy of history followed in its train. Heidegger was especially impressed by Wilhelm Dilthey (1833–1911), whose collected works began to appear in 1913. As well as being a historian of culture, Dilthey tried to do for history what Kant had done for the natural sciences, to spell out the basic *a priori* conditions that enable us to study history. Another significant figure, whom Heidegger often mentions in his early lectures though not in BT itself, is Oswald Spengler (1880–1936). In *The Decline of the West* (2 vols, 1918, 1922) Spengler presented the past as a series of distinct, self-contained cultures, each of which undergoes, like a living organism, a process of growth, maturity, and decay. Thought and values are, on Spengler's view, always relative to a specific culture and have no universal validity. Even mathematics is culturally determined: ancient Greek mathematics is significantly different from modern mathematics, and not simply an incomplete fragment of it.

This problem of historical relativism concerned Heidegger as well as many other philosophers of the time. In his early lectures he quotes Eduard Spranger:

> All of us – Rickert, the phenomenologists, the tendency that starts with Dilthey – we all come together in the great struggle over the timeless in the historical, over the realm of sense and its expression in a concrete culture that has arisen, over a theory of values which leads beyond the merely subjective to objective validity.
>
> (xxi. 91; lxiii. 42)

Heidegger does not like Spranger's way of putting it: he dislikes talk about 'values' and the 'realm of sense', dubbing it 'platonism for barbarians' (xxi. 91). But he agrees that relativism is a problem, and argues that there have so far been three types of solution to it. One is Spengler's, to give free rein to the historical and accept that there is no suprahistorical objectivity, nothing that is as true in 1927 as it was in 500 BCE. Another is Platonism, the attempt to extract eternal truths and values from varying historical contexts, if not to ignore history altogether. Spranger favours this solution. So do Descartes and Husserl. Descartes despised history, since it lacked the certainty of mathematics and physics. Husserl was hardly interested in history, even the history of philosophy. Philosophy, on his view as on Descartes's, is based on intuitively evident truths that can in principle be discerned at any time. The history of ideas is irrelevant to their truth. The third solution is a 'compromise' between the first two – Heidegger associates it with Georg Simmel (1858–1918): it 'acknowledges a minimum of absolute values, but they are embodied in the historical context only in a relative form' (lx. 48).

None of these solutions suits Heidegger. There are, he insists, no compromises in philosophy to get us to the heart of the matter. The philosopher is always a 'beginner' (lxi. 13). Nor are there any evident truths discernible without regard to our historical context. Husserl's distinction between 'factuality' and 'validity' is a 'banal platonism' (xvii. 94). It ignores the fact that our present situation, the situation in which we discern whatever truths we do, is steeped in the historical tradition. History is not dead and gone, history is what we are (xvii. 114). Hence the contrast between systematic philosophy and the history of philosophy is spurious. The history of philosophy essentially concerns the present. We need to study it to free ourselves of the inadequate categories that it has bequeathed to us. Conversely, we need to engage in systematic philosophy too, to equip ourselves with a fore-having, a fore-sight, and a fore-conception, if we are to make sense of the history of philosophy. This applies to history of any kind. I need some prior view of the past if I am to appreciate a historical source, such as a document or a coin (lviii. 204). Historical remnants alone do not make us historians: we must be equipped to see them *as* evidence of some past event. This prior equipment belongs to the present.

Previous philosophers of history – the Platonists, Spengler, and the compromisers – made three connected mistakes. They neglect the intertwining of the past with the present. They view the historical past only through the eyes of historians, history as pre-packaged by historiography. They neglect Dasein and Dasein's intrinsic historicality. Individual Dasein tends to be dissolved into a culture: 'Rickert says that the human individual in its uniqueness is no more than what it has contributed to cultural values. Here the concept of the individual is conceived purely platonically' (lx. 50). Or into humanity: Dilthey 'persists in the traditional view of history, which I regard as the aesthetic view of history governed by the idea of humanity' (xvii. 92). Once Dasein comes back into its own, we see the continuity between the past and the present. History is the history of past Dasein and its world, not of anonymous cultures or periods quite distinct from our own.

Happening, History, and Fate

The word 'history' refers both to events, especially past events, and to the study or narration of such events. German has two words corresponding to 'history', *Historie* and *Geschichte*. Both are similarly ambiguous. But Heidegger reserves *Historie* for the study or narration of past events, 'historiography' or 'historiology'. *Geschichte* is used for the history that *Historie* studies, though Heidegger prefers to consider it independently of *Historie*. The words 'historical' (*geschichtlich*) and 'historicality' (*Geschichtlichkeit*) stem from *Geschichte*. Two other words related to *Geschichte* are *Schicksal*, 'fate', and *Geschick*, 'destiny'. But these words, like *Geschichte* itself, derive ultimately from *geschehen*, an ordinary word for 'happen' or 'occur', but often translated as 'historize' in Heidegger's texts, to capture its affinity to *Geschichte*.

These concepts – history, happening, fate – seem quite diverse, if we disregard the contingencies of German word-formation. How do they fit together? Let us start with happening or 'historizing', since that is apparently the simplest of these concepts. What *happens*? Dasein *happens*. Dasein stretches itself out between its birth and its death, and the 'specific movement in which Dasein is stretched along and stretches itself along, we call its "historizing"' (BT, 375). Dasein does not happen as a sequence of momentary experiences borne by a persisting subject. It happens by running ahead to its own death and returning to its birth, by resolutely choosing one of its possibilities in the present 'moment of vision', and by adhering to it in 'self-constancy'. This possibility is Dasein's fate:

> Once one has grasped the finitude of one's existence, it snatches one back from the endless multiplicity of possibilities which offer themselves as closest to one – those of comfortableness, shirking, and taking things lightly – and brings Dasein into the simplicity of its fate.
>
> (BT, 384)

Only someone who has a fate in this sense can suffer at the hands of fate in the external sense. An irresolute person who drifts with the tide may have bad luck, but he cannot suffer the blows of fate. 'Fate' is different from 'destiny':

> But if fateful Dasein, as Being-in-the-world, exists essentially in Being with Others, its historizing is a co-historizing and is determinative for it as destiny. This is how we designate the historizing of the community, of a people.
>
> (BT, 384)

Destiny is not simply the aggregate of the fates of separate individuals. Our fates are orchestrated into a single destiny by our interaction in a common world with a shared history:

> Only in communicating and in struggling does the power of destiny become free. Dasein's fateful destiny in and with its 'generation' goes to make up the full authentic historizing of Dasein.
>
> (BT, 384f.)

Heidegger tries to steer a course between extreme individualism and complete absorption in the *they*.

'Some talk of Alexander, and some of Hercules'

Running ahead to death frees Dasein from the grip of *them* and ensures the authenticity of its resolve. But it does not of itself tell Dasein what to do or even supply it with a range of possibilities for its fate. For this, Dasein must return to the past, perhaps to its own birth, but more likely beyond. There an expanse of possibilities is opened up. There are great philosophers, generals, statesmen, artists, saints, and lovers, whose deeds and works are part of Dasein's heritage. There are also humble sextons like Heidegger's father; heroes come in all shapes and sizes. Dasein should 'repeat' or 'retrieve' such a possibility, it should 'choose its hero' (BT, 385). To repeat a possibility does not mean to reproduce it exactly. I cannot reproduce the campaigns of Alexander; I could copy word for word the texts of Plato, but this would be both pointless and unplatonic. Repetition is more like a conversation with the past or with some past hero. Alexander or Plato make certain suggestions to me, in their own deeds and works, and I make a rejoinder to them. In doing so, I disavow 'that which in the "today" is working itself out as the "past"' (BT, 438); I disown the possibilities and interpretations presented to me by *them*.

Dasein does not have an unlimited choice of heroes. The French Revolutionaries may have tried to emulate ancient rebels and republicans. Napoleon may have proposed a rejoinder to Alexander or Caesar. But most people opt for one of the roles handed down from the immediate past – a shoemaker, a priest, a sexton. Heidegger selected his heroes from among philosophers. Aristotle, or perhaps Brentano, first induced him to become a philosopher rather than a sexton, a priest, or a soldier. Aristotle too guides his attempts to do philosophy, though other philosophers – Plato, Kant, and so on – are also called into play. Dasein need not choose only one hero. Nor even just one type of hero: Heidegger later invokes poets such as Hölderlin and Rilke. He repeats them. But this means that he interprets them – armed with his own fore-having, fore-sight, and fore-conception – argues with them, replies to them, confronting them with the problems and solutions current in his own day, but abandoning or reworking these problems and solutions in view of his engagement with the past. In later works he explicitly presents himself as engaged in a 'conversation' with thinkers and poets of the past. This is Heidegger's fate. How does it play its part in a destiny? Napoleon's fate is part of the destiny of France. Heidegger's fate belongs to the destinies of progressively wider communities. It belongs to the destiny of his pupils and followers, of Freiburg University, of the German people, and perhaps ultimately of what he later called 'the West'. Must Napoleon's followers each have a fate, as well as Napoleon, if France is to have a destiny? Must Heidegger's pupils be as resolute as Heidegger himself, or is it enough if they take his word for it? How many Germans need to be resolutely authentic on their own account? If only it were as easy as Heidegger supposes to distinguish a destiny from *them*!

Inauthentic Historicality

So far we have described authentic historicality, the historicality of resolute Dasein. Mostly Dasein is not resolute, but it is nevertheless historical. Its historicality differs from that of authentic Dasein in two respects. First, since it does not run ahead to its death and revert to its birth, does not abide in self-constancy by a resolution formed in a moment of vision, it seems more like a series of distinct experiences strung out along a persisting subject. This gives rise to what Heidegger regards as a bogus problem: What is it about these experiences that connects them together as the experiences of a single person? Secondly, irresolute Dasein derives its view of history and the past more from the objects of its daily concern than authentic Dasein does. That is, history becomes world-history. But 'world-history' is an ambiguous term. In one sense, even authentic historicality is world-history, since what is historical is not Dasein on its own, not a worldless subject, but Dasein in a world. In another sense 'world-history' refers not to the historicality of Dasein, but to the historicality of items within the world – of tools, books, buildings, even nature 'as a countryside, as an area that has been colonized or exploited, as a battlefield, or as the site of a cult' (BT, 388f.). As ever, inauthentic, fallen Dasein is dispersed in the world of the present: 'Lost in the making present of the "today", it understands the "past" in terms of the "Present"' (BT, 391) – and not, as authentic Dasein does, in terms of the future, of its own fate.

The meaning of inauthentic historicality becomes clearer if we consider Heidegger's own fate, the practice of philosophy. What does a philosopher do if his existence is inauthentically historical? He may, on the one hand, be a purely 'systematic' philosopher, concerned with current ideas to the exclusion of the history of the subject. 'With the inconstancy of the theyself Dasein makes present its "today". In awaiting the next new thing, it has already forgotten the old one' (BT, 391). He is oblivious to the *history* of current ideas: 'it is loaded down with the legacy of a "past" which has become unrecognizable, and it seeks the modern' (BT, 391). On the other hand, an inauthentically historical philosopher may be interested in the history of philosophy, in the texts of past philosophers. An interest in history is no guarantee of authentic historicality. To see why this is so, we need to look at Heidegger's account of *Historie*, of 'historiology'.

From Historicality to Historiology

Dasein is invariably historical, though often it is only inauthentically historical. Not all Dasein is historiological, interested in the explicit study of history, nor are all ages. Authentic 'historicality does not necessarily require historiology. It is not the case that unhistoriological eras as such are unhistorical also' (IST, 396). Heidegger has in mind the ancient Greeks, who, though they produced the first serious historians – Herodotus and Thucydides – were not so intensely interested in their past as the Romans were, let alone the Germans of the nineteenth century. They were entitled to neglect the history of philosophy, at least, since they were beginners or originators of the subject, free of the burden of philosophical tradition that weighs on us. The Greeks made history with more ardour than they studied it.

Nevertheless historiology is rooted in Dasein's historicality. Historiology, like all sciences, presupposes a prior disclosure of the realm that it then 'thematizes'. It also presupposes the present survival of remnants of a past world – documents, buildings, skeletons, and so on. But they will not be treated as historical evidence unless we regard them as 'world-historical':

> Our going back to 'the past' does not first get its start from the
> acquisition, sifting, and securing of such material; these activities
> presuppose historical Being towards the Dasein that has-been-there –
> that is, they presuppose the historicality of the historian's existence.
>
> (BT, 394)

Dasein has 'historical being to the Dasein that has been there' in that
it chooses a role from among those it inherits from the recent past.
But even in its unhistoriological mode, Dasein is familiar with various
figures and events of the past. We know that Caesar crossed the
Rubicon, even if we do not know why he did so or where the Rubicon
is. When we see ourselves as making a significant and irrevocable
choice – a choice to marry, say, which though less momentous than
Caesar's, is significant for one's own life – we often speak or think of
ourselves as crossing the Rubicon. In a way, we then 'repeat' Caesar's
action. The historian too makes choices and is likely to appeal to the
past in making them. If he is, say, a politician, the problems he faces
and the choices he makes in his political life will affect his selection of a
historical theme: 'The "selection" of what is to become a possible
object for historiology has already been met with in the factical
existentiell choice of Dasein's historicality' (BT, 395). Macaulay's
decision to write a history of England from the accession of James II
was influenced by his championship of the 1831 Reform Bill and of other
progressive causes. Augustine's history of Rome, in the City of God,
was inspired by Alaric's sacking of Rome together with his own
resolute devotion to Christianity.

Historiology and Dasein's Possibilities

How does the authentically historical historian approach the past?
Dasein exists, it chooses its way of being from the possibilities available
to it. This is how the historian views himself, and it is how he views the
past Dasein that he studies. He will be concerned not simply with what
past Dasein actually did or did not do, but with the possibilities

available to it, what it could have chosen as well as what it did choose, and also with the possibilities that it hands down to us. The authentic historian tells us not simply that Caesar crossed the Rubicon and what resulted from this. He tells us that Caesar faces at this stage of his career three possibilities. He can remain in Gaul with his army; then his enemies in Rome will ensure that he receives no more supplies and reinforcements, so that he will eventually be reduced to impotence. He can return to Rome without his army; then his enemies will kill him. Or he can illegally cross into Italy with his army; then there will be a civil war.

A statesman or a general might study Caesar's situation for the possibilities that it opens up to himself, for the bearing it has on his own situation. But again it is easier to see what Heidegger has in mind if we consider the history of philosophy. A philosopher does not simply make certain claims. He makes choices, choosing this possibility rather than that. Descartes responded to scepticism by attempting to rebuild the edifice of knowledge by arguing carefully from self-evident premises. But other responses are possible – that of Montaigne, for instance, who argued that if everything is uncertain, then Protestantism is uncertain, so that one may as well stick to traditional Catholicism. A reader of Descartes (Kierkegaard, say) may prefer one of those possibilities that he neglected. Or a reader (say, Schopenhauer) of Plato's *Republic*, which argues that art lies at two removes from the true forms or ideas – since it copies the ordinary objects which are themselves copies of the ideas – may wonder at Plato's neglect of another, and perhaps preferable, possibility – that art directly depicts ideas. Again, in the first edition of his *Critique of Pure Reason* Kant broached the possibility that our faculties of sensibility and understanding are both rooted in imagination; in the second edition he abandoned this idea and reinstated the primacy of reason. Heidegger preferred the possibility rejected by Kant, that man is an imaginative being rather than a primarily rational being. (This does not mean that Heidegger was an *irrationalist*: 'When irrationalism . . . talks about the things to which rationalism is blind, it does so only with a squint' (BT, 136).) Past philosophers are to be read with a view to their possibilities – possibilities chosen, rejected, suppressed, but all of them left to us.

Nietzsche's Possibilities

Heidegger concludes his chapter on history with some illustrations of this approach to the subject. In the second of his *Untimely Meditations*, 'On the Use and Abuse of History for Life' (1874), Nietzsche distinguished three types of historiology: the monumental (which portrays the glories of the past as an inspiration to the present and the future), the antiquarian (which records the past for its own sake), and the critical (which censures the blemishes of the past). Why just three possibilities? And are they alternatives? Nietzsche, Heidegger suggests, 'understood more than he has made known to us' (BT, 396), and in view of Dasein's temporality all three are involved in authentic historiology. As resolutely futural, Dasein is 'open for the "monumental" possibilities of human existence' (BT, 396), and this gives rise to monumental historiology. But since Dasein is also 'thrown', it has the 'possibility of reverently preserving the existence that has-been-there', the existence which revealed to it the possibility it has chosen. This is antiquarian historiology. Dasein also has to make its choice in the present, but not the present as *they* interpret it. Authentic historiology is 'a way of painfully detaching oneself from the falling publicness of the "today"', and so, as well as being monumental and antiquarian, it is also a 'critique of the "Present"' (BT, 397). Nietzsche, when read in the right way, confirms Heidegger's own account of history.

Dasein which has been there

Nietzsche was dead when BT appeared. So was Descartes, and many of the other philosophers Heidegger considered. Husserl (1859–1938) was still alive. Yet Heidegger treats Husserl in much the same way as

Descartes: they are both 'possibilities of the being of care' (xvii. 107). Does it matter to historicality whether other Dasein is dead or alive? Sometimes Heidegger suggests that it does. Artefacts are historical because they were 'used by a concernful Dasein who was-in-the-world. That world is no longer' (BT, 280). Hence historiology deals with Dasein that has been there, and, since Dasein is being-in-the-world, that involves world-history: 'If Dasein is there no longer, then the world too is something that has-been-there' (BT, 393). Dasein's world dies along with Dasein, Heidegger implies. This is puzzling. Two contemporaries are each in-the-world. But they are in the same world. Why can I not be in the same world as someone was who is now dead? In any case, contemporaries do not conveniently die at the same time, nor need they all be dead before we write the history of their exploits: there are still survivors of the World Wars. We need to distinguish between 'having been there' and 'being no longer there'. What matters to Heidegger as a historical being is that Husserl has been there: Husserl's texts were ('always already') on hand from his schooldays, like those of Descartes. It makes no difference from this point of view, though it may from others, that Husserl is still around, alive and kicking, available for questioning and ready to answer back, in a way that Descartes is not. Can Dasein's historicality give us the idea of an objective temporal order, in which Descartes lived and died before the birth of Kant, who in turn died before Husserl was born? Perhaps. As Heidegger scans the pages of Descartes he finds no mention of Kant or Husserl, whereas Husserl refers often to Descartes and Kant. Were they each in a different world? This is less plausible with regard to their thought than other aspects of their life. Kant's philosophy is less out of date than his wig. But to place them in their chronological order, let alone give the dates of their births and deaths, we need to assign them to the same world and to the same world-time.

World-Time

Time is 'significant'. Dasein needs time for doing things, it takes time to do things, it can 'lose' or waste time. This depends on Dasein's being as care, its temporality, and its finitude:

> The 'there' is disclosed in a way which is grounded in Dasein's own temporality as ecstatically stretched along, and with this disclosure a 'time' is allotted to Dasein; only because of this can Dasein, as factically thrown, 'take' its time and lose it.
>
> (BT, 410)

The *significance* of time is more fundamental than time-reckoning or time-measurement. I look at my watch because I need to get to a meeting on time. I look at my diary because I am wondering whether I shall meet my deadline. I would not consult watches or diaries if I did not need time to do things, if I did not need to do things on time.

Corresponding to the three ecstases of temporality there are, in German, three temporal adverbs: 'then' (*dann*) referring to a future time, 'now' (*jetzt*) referring to the present, and 'then' or 'on that former occasion' (*damals*) referring to a past time. We use these in planning: I must dress *now* before the cab arrives *then*; I must resit the exam which I failed *then* on that former occasion. Both 'then' and 'on that former occasion' involve 'now'; 'then' implies 'now-not-yet', and 'on that former occasion' implies 'now-no-longer'; the cab is not yet here, and I am not failing my exam *now*. Temporality 'ensnares itself in the Present, which, in making present, says pre-eminently "Now! Now!"' (BT, 407).

The 'now', 'then', and 'on that former occasion' are 'datable'. We assign a time to worldly events: 'then, when the cab arrives', 'now that you are dressed', 'then, when you failed the exam'. This is related to time's significance: we could not plan our activities temporally, unless we could assign times to them. Time is also 'spanned' or extended. We refer not primarily to instants but to the time in between: 'I'll read until the cab comes', 'I've worked ever since I failed the exam'. Even the present is not a durationless instant, but a shorter or longer span of time: ' "now" – in the intermission, while one is eating, in the evening, in summer' (BT, 409). This is related to datability. What we do, and what happens, takes time – we cannot do anything in a durationless instant. Time is public. This too is related to datability. Often we date the same time by different events. The time that for me is *then, when* I married is for you *then, when* you left school. But usually we manage to sort this out and date a time by an event known to us both: I married, and you left school, *then, when* England last won the World Cup. We co-ordinate our actions in public time: we arrange to meet *then, when* the concert ends.

Life is made easier by clocks. The natural, primeval clock is the sun, by whose light we see to perform our daily tasks. The sun is there for everyone in the same longitude. It is not attached to any particular person or business. We measure time, initially, by the movement of the sun: 'because the temporality of the Dasein which must take its time is finite, its days are already numbered' (BT, 413). We measure time because there is a right time and a wrong time for doing things. Like the world, time is *significant*. Hence time becomes worldly, world-time, a time within which everything present at hand or ready to hand has its place. Later, when we become less dependent on sunlight for our activities, we devise clocks that do not require sunlight – though they must keep in time, more or less, with the movements of the sun.

'Ordinary Time'

Measurement, as it becomes more refined, alters our conception of time. It stresses the present at the expense of the other ecstases. A runner in a race does not focus primarily on the present. He looks ahead to the moment when he will cross the finishing-line to the applause of the spectators. He gears himself up for the final sprint. All this is lost on the person timing his run. *Now*, at 3 o'clock by his watch, the runner sets off; *now*, at 3.05, he is half-way; *now*, at 3.10, he crosses the finishing-line. The timer is not wholly oblivious to the past and the future. He 'retains' the start of the run at 3.00, and awaits its completion. But retention and waiting are muffled by the imperious presence of the now.

Time measured is still spanned. The race *lasts* 10 minutes, from 3.00 to 3.10. But the *now* is not spanned. The race begins now, at exactly 3.00, not in a long-drawn-out now, as when a spectator says 'It's going to begin now'. And it ends at exactly 3.10. The present of time-measurement is, ideally at least, not spanned.

Time is still public and it is still significant. I am timing a runner, and the time of his run is articulated by its phases; the time, like the run, has a beginning, a middle, and an end. Other spectators see the race and their watches, perhaps, say the same as mine. But the time-measurer is more engrossed in the movements of his watch, and less in events in the world, than the runner or an excited spectator in periods of boredom clocks can take complete control. As I wait for a train on an empty station, time seems entirely empty and homogeneous, punctuated by nothing except the movements of the clock. It is not related to any significant events; it seems to be an entity in its own right.

This, Heidegger argues, gives rise to Aristotle's view of time, as a sequence of nows. Shorn of its datability and significance, ecstatic temporality gets 'levelled off' (BT, 422), so that time is homogeneous. The nows are seen as present-at-hand, and time is almost a thing among other things. Now-time is uninterrupted and has no gaps – unlike ecstatic temporality, which glides over periods in which nothing is happening. It is infinite – a feature which Heidegger attributes to a 'fleeing in the face of death' (BT, 424). It is thoroughly public: it 'belongs to everybody – and that means, to nobody' (BT, 425). Nevertheless, now-time still bears marks of its origin in temporality. Time is said to pass away, rather than to arise: 'Dasein knows fugitive time in terms of its "fugitive" knowledge about its death' (BT, 425). It is also irreversible, moving irrevocably in one direction, and this can be explained only in terms of its derivation from ecstatic temporality. It makes little difference to the timer of the race if the race runs backwards, or even if his watch runs backwards; he can still time the race. But it cannot be so for the runner himself, looking ahead to the finishing-line, with victory in his grasp but not yet fully assured. Now-time, then, derives from ecstatic temporality. Conversely, it would be difficult, perhaps impossible, to construct ecstatic temporality out of the impoverished now-time, however much we plaster it over with significance and value.

Now-time is derivative. It does not follow that it is unreal or illegitimate: 'The ordinary representation of time has its natural justification' (BT, 426). Historiology requires world-time, if not now-time: 'Temporality temporalizes world-time, within the horizon of which "history" can "appear" as historizing within-time' (BT, 436). Heidegger does not want us to discard world-time in favour of ecstatic temporality. That would deprive us of the stable framework within which resoluteness operates. Authenticity, resoluteness, ecstatic temporality – these enable me to grapple with the texts of Aristotle and to propose, say, that the original meaning of 'truth' was 'unconcealment'. Inauthenticity, fallenness, world-time – these enable me to speak, for the most part, contemporary English and to say that Aristotle died in 322 BCE. Here as elsewhere inauthenticity serves its purpose.

Heidegger versus Hegel

In the penultimate section of BT Heidegger argues that Hegel (1770–1831) accepted Aristotle's conception of time and did not go far beyond

it. Why Hegel? In part it is because Heidegger had immense respect for
Hegel,

> who saw and was able to see in philosophy so much more than had ever
> been seen before, because he had an uncommon power over language
> and wrested concealed things from their hiding-places.
>
> (xxiv. 226)

In part it is because Hegel seems to anticipate some of Heidegger's
central doctrines and strategies. Hegel's *Phenomenology of Spirit*
(1807) can readily be seen as a rejection of traditional epistemology
in favour of ontology, that is, an exploration of the being of the
knower and the known, and of the relationship between them. But
Heidegger won't have it. For him Hegel is the last and greatest of
the Cartesians; the supreme rationalist, who dissolved ontology into
logic; the overweening metaphysician, who saw man as infinite,
destined to view reality through the eye of God. So Heidegger
takes issue with Hegel – both to remove a monstrous obstacle
on the path to truth and to make sure that no one confuses
Heidegger with Hegel.

'The rest is silence'

One trait Heidegger shares with Hegel is a tendency not to finish the
books he promised to write. Hegel's *Phenomenology* was originally
published as the first part of a system, to be followed by a volume
dealing with logic, philosophy of nature, and philosophy of mind. The
second part of this system never appeared. Heidegger must have been
aware of this when he left BT incomplete, but kept the words 'First
Half' on the title-page until 1953. Did he hope to invite comparison
between Hegel's *Phenomenology* and his own BT, the one recording the
voyage of consciousness (*Bewusstsein*) through its various 'forms', the
other exploring ever-deeper levels of the being of Dasein, behind the
masks of its self-interpretations?

No doubt we should suggest some more substantial reason for Heidegger's failure to continue BT. He ends with the question 'Does time itself manifest itself as the horizon of Being?' (BT, 437). His idea seems to be that in view of our new understanding of time, we can now consider being in general, disregarding particular modes of being and disregarding its relationship to Dasein. More than once he has indicated that Dasein can only be analysed properly if 'the ontology of possible entities within-the-world is oriented securely enough by clarifying the idea of Being in general' (BT, 366). We might doubt whether BT leaves much of interest to be said on this matter. It is, first, not obvious that we need to elucidate being in general to understand the differences between various modes of being, between rocks, tools, Dasein, time, and world. Heidegger thinks of being in general as a 'horizon' for differentiating modes of being, a vantage point beyond any particular type of entity from which we can survey and discriminate their varieties and interrelations. But even if finite Dasein can attain such a vantage point, what might there be of interest to say about it? Secondly, Heidegger seems to have closed off the route to Dasein-independent being, or to a vantage point beyond Dasein itself, by his persistent claim that there is no being *without* Dasein. BT has not focused on the being of Dasein to the exclusion of other entities. Time, world, hammers, rocks – all these are interpreted by Dasein in their being. What more can there be to being than what Dasein makes of all this?

Did Heidegger's thought end with BT? Naturally not. He writes on different themes. Often he seems to contradict BT, sometimes he denies that he does so. It needs no special explanation that in a literary career of fifty-odd years Heidegger did not continually rework the same themes and that he occasionally changed his mind. What is remarkable, and no doubt owes something to his 'resoluteness', is his attempt to integrate all his work into a single coherent whole. But rather than ask how coherent it really is, it is better to consider a sample of his later work on a theme that hardly appears in BT: art.

Chapter 10
Art

Heidegger showed little interest in art until the mid-1930s, and then it appears in the company of several related interests: the presocratic philosophers, whose works are often in poetic form and are more closely related to Greek poetry than, say, Kant is to German poetry; philosophers such as Schelling and Nietzsche, for whom art has a central position in philosophy; and language, which, for Heidegger, originates with poets.

Artworks and Things

Heidegger's most general work on art, 'The Origin of the Work of Art', was published in 1950, but stems from lectures given in 1935. He rejects two widely held doctrines. First, that art is concerned only with beauty and pleasure: 'art is rather the disclosure of the being of beings' (IM, 111). Second, that a work of art is primarily a thing, and that aesthetic value is superimposed on it by our subjective view of it: for Heidegger it is art that shows us what a thing is. There are nevertheless two ways in which an artwork is a thing. First, a work, such as a painting, can be moved and stored like other things. (He later rejects this way of viewing artworks. It treats them as objects present at hand, in the way that an art-dealer or a removal-man does.) Second, it has a thingly aspect: 'There is something stony in a work of architecture, wooden in a carving, coloured in a painting, spoken in a linguistic work, sonorous in a musical composition' (OWA, 19).

What then is a thing? There are three traditional accounts: a thing is (1) a bearer of properties; (2) the unity of perceptual sensations; or (3) a composite of form and matter. Heidegger rejects (1) and (2), the latter for the reason that 'we never really first perceive the throng of sensations . . . We hear the door shut in the house and never hear acoustical sensations or even mere sounds' (OWA, 26). He prefers (3), the form-matter account. This was originally derived from, and is best suited to, intrinsically useful equipment such as a jug or shoes. But equipment is only one of three types of thing: a 'mere thing' such as a rock, equipment, and an artwork. An artwork differs from equipment and has something in common with a mere thing. Like a natural rock and unlike shoes, an artwork is not produced for a specific use or purpose, though unlike the rock and shoes it is not 'self-contained' (OWA, 29): it calls for an observer or interpreter. Still, since the tradition gives priority to equipment, Heidegger decides to look at that first.

Van Gogh's Shoes

He does this by introducing his first exhibit: Van Gogh's painting of a solitary pair of worn peasant shoes. We cannot just look at the shoes we are wearing, because attention distorts our view of them: shoes are essentially inconspicuous to their wearer. From the painting, Heidegger argues, we see that the shoes are involved both with the world – the world of human products and activities – and with the earth – the natural foundation on which the world rests. This is overlooked *both* by the ordinary user *and* by the form-matter theory. Owing to their excessive familiarity, the user regards his shoes as simply things for walking. Or (to take a different example) someone familiar with a cricket bat regards it as a piece of wood for hitting balls. The form-matter theory refines this account. Focusing on the *manufacture* of shoes and bats, it says that shoes and bats are pieces of matter (leather, nails, wood) with a form (their usefulness) imposed on them. The user and the theory neglect much else that would need to be

8. *Shoes*, a painting by Vincent van Gogh

explained to an uninformed alien: the involvement of the shoes with the world of the peasant, and the wear and tear they undergo from earth; the involvement of the bat with the world of cricket (stumps, bowlers, etc.) and the earth on which it is planted. But what they neglect becomes apparent in the painting: 'the equipmentality of equipment first genuinely arrives at its appearance through the work . . . The nature of art would then be this: the truth of beings setting itself to work' (OWA, 36). The work is not a thing with artistic qualities added: the work reveals the nature of things.

The Greek Temple

Heidegger now presents his second exhibit: a Greek temple. He does so partly to distinguish his own view from the view that art is imitation: the temple is not representational. But partly also because he wants to argue that a work of art not only opens up a world; it also sets up a world, a world to which it belongs. The Van Gogh opens up the world of the peasant. But it does not set it up, nor does it belong there. The temple, by contrast, unifies and articulates the world of a people: it 'first fits together and at the same time gathers around itself the unity of those paths and relations in which birth and death, disaster and blessing, victory and disgrace, endurance and decline acquire the shape of destiny for human being' (OWA, 42). The world of a people is the familiar structured realm in which they know their way about and make their decisions.

The temple not only sets *up* world. It sets *forth* world's counterpart, earth. It is surrounded by 'earthy' nature, buffeted by storms and resting on rock, and it also consists of earthy natural materials. It thus reveals earth as earth, and grounds the world on earth. All artworks set forth earth in their way. In equipment, earthy raw materials are 'used up', that is, fused into the artefact so that they are no longer noticeable: it does not matter, and we do not notice, whether shoes are made of leather or of some functionally equivalent material. In artworks materials are only 'used', not 'used up': they remain conspicuous within the work (OWA, 47f.). The earthy materials of poetry, the poet's words, are, unlike the words of common discourse, conspicuous and resistant to paraphrase. It matters whether the Parthenon is made of marble or plastic. In one way or another, all artworks set forth earth.

World is the human environment in which we lead our lives: the tools we use, the houses we dwell in, the values we invoke. Earth is the natural setting of this world, the ground on which it rests and the source of raw materials for our artefacts. World and earth are opposites in conflict. World strives for clarity and openness, while earth shelters and conceals, tending to draw world into itself. Each needs and sustains the other. The artwork straddles both contestants. The temple's static repose is the product of the conflict between earth and world. It is a happening, an event – the event of truth as

119

9. The Temple of Aphaia in Aegina, *c*.500 BCE

unconcealment. Only if beings are unconcealed can we make particular conjectures and decisions. But since we finite creatures never wholly master beings cognitively or practically, there is also concealment. Without concealment there would be no objectivity, no decisions, and no history: everything, the past, the present, and the future, would be wholly transparent to us, leaving no hidden depths to things, and no scope for choices with uncertain outcomes. (The two pairs of opposites, earth–world and concealment–unconcealment, do not exactly coincide. Earth is partly unconcealed, and the world is partly concealed.) Truth happens in the work: 'Setting up a world and setting forth the earth, the work is the fighting of the battle in which the unconcealedness of beings as a whole, or truth, is won' (OWA, 55).

Heidegger plays down the role of the artist and tends to regard the work as the product of an impersonal force, such as truth or art itself, that uses the artist to actualize itself. In 'great art' the artist effaces himself: he is like a 'passageway that destroys itself in the creative process for the work to emerge' (OWA, 40). But an artwork is essentially 'created' (OWA, 56f.). Creation is quite distinct from the manufacture of a tool: art is not craftsmanship plus something extra, any more than a work is a tool plus something extra.

Art and Truth

Why must truth happen in a work? The conflict between concealment and unconcealment is a conflict between an old paradigm and a new paradigm, between, say, an old religion and a new religion. An artwork is like a fortress or standard marking the ground newly won for truth: 'Clearing [*Lichtung*] of openness and establishment in the Open belong together' (OWA, 61). There are, Heidegger concedes (OWA, 62), other ways of staking our claim to truth: an 'act that founds a political state' (e.g. the US Constitution); the 'nearness of that which is not simply a being, but the being that is most of all' (e.g. the conversion of St Paul); the essential sacrifice (e.g. the Crucifixion); or the thinker's questioning. (Science is not an 'original happening of truth'. It fills in the details of a 'domain of truth already opened . . . [I]nsofar as a science passes beyond correctness and goes on to a truth, . . . it is philosophy'.) But art is the main way in which truth happens. Not only the temple but also Greek tragedy lay down the paradigm, the values and categories, in terms of which a people view the world and make their choices.

Why must the artwork be created? A work involves a 'rift' between earth and world, and (unlike equipment) composes conspicuous earthy materials into a reposeful form. The notion of rift, *Riss*, links up with that of a ground-plan or paradigm, a *Grundriss* (OWA, 64). But it also means that a work is conspicuous, owing to the tension it embodies. A broom fades into the background of other equipment, its constituent materials 'used up', smoothed down into its usefulness. A work is solitary, tensed, and striking. It is especially suitable as a marker of truth. But the very existence of the work cries out for explanation. A work, unlike a tool, bears the scars of its production. The rift needs a creator to contain it.

A work needs an audience or 'preservers' as well as a creator. The work draws its preservers 'out of the realm of the ordinary' into the new world it opens up, and suspends their 'usual doing and valuing, knowing and looking' (OWA, 66). The appropriate response to a work is neither knowing nor willing, but a 'knowing that remains a willing, and willing that remains a knowing' (OWA, 67). It is not carrying out some plan one has already formed, but 'resoluteness', the ecstatic entry into a new realm of openness in which all one's old beliefs and desires are suspended. It is somewhat like St Paul's conversion, opening up a new field for knowing and willing that is disconnected from one's previous notions and plans. Great art, like the voice of God, is not consumer-led: it changes one's whole way of viewing the world and of finding one's way about in it. But the work is not like a drug, and the experience is not private: the work is communal and grounds our relations to one another.

A work, Heidegger has said, is not a thing or a tool with something added; things, stuffs, are inconspicuous in equipment and revealed only in works. But what about the artist? Must not he know about nature, about the things and tools he portrays, before he creates art? No. It is the work that draws out the rift (*Riss*) and draws the sketch (*Riss*) (OWA, 70). The artist does not *first* have a clear view of things and *then* embody it in a work: nature is opened up for him, as well as for us, only in the work. The work needs creators, who 'put truth into the work', and also preservers, who 'put it to work', actualize it, that is, in their communal knowing-willing (OWA, 71). But the work also makes creators, as well as preservers, *possible*. Creators are agents of a force larger than themselves: art.

Truth comes, in a way, from nothing. We cannot account for Van Gogh's painting by supposing that he came across some old shoes, and painted what he saw. For, first, the shoes alone could not account for the way in which Van Gogh saw them. And secondly, he did not see them in a new way *before* his painting emerged: 'the opening up of the

Open, and the clearing of beings, happens only as the openness is projected' (OWA, 71). Art, like St Paul's conversion, comes as a bolt from the blue.

Poetry

All art, then, is essentially *Dichtung* (OWA, 72). *Dichtung* here has a wide sense and means something like 'invention' or 'projection'. What the artist puts into the work is not derived from the things around him but invented or projected. All great art involves a 'change . . . of the unconcealment of beings' (OWA, 72): it illuminates the ordinary, it rips us for a time out of the ordinary into another world, or it changes our whole view of the world. In a narrow sense, however, *Dichtung* means 'poetry' (*Poesio*), and poetry is Heidegger's third exhibit. He does not believe that all other arts are, or stem from, poetry. What he believes is this. Language is not just a medium for communicating what we know. Language used for this purpose is 'actual language at any given moment'. Language also brings beings out of 'dim confusion' into the open by naming them for the first time, and thus gives us something to communicate about. This is innovative language or 'projective saying' (OWA, 74). It lays down what can and what cannot be said in the language of communication. Since poetry is in language, and since it is a form of art, that is, of the lighting projection of truth, poetry must be projective saying, an original, innovative use of language to name things and thus open up a realm in which we can communicate.

Poetry is not, however, only one among several arts. The other arts – architecture, sculpture, painting, music – operate within a realm already opened up by language. The disclosure effected by language, that is, by poetry, preceded disclosure by the other arts. So poetry is prior to the other arts, just as linguistic disclosure is prior to other forms of disclosure.

The Founding of Truth

All art is *dichterisch*, inventive or projective. So too is the preservation of a work, since the preserver has to enter the realm disclosed by the work. But the essence of *Dichtung*, Heidegger continues, is the founding of truth. 'Founding', *Stiftung*, has three senses, and art involves founding in all three senses. First, 'bestowing'. The setting into (the) work of truth involves a paradigm-shift: it thrusts up the extraordinary and thrusts down the ordinary. So truth cannot derive from what went before. It comes as a *gift*. Founding is an 'overflow', the bestowal of a gift (OWA, 75).

Second, founding is 'grounding'. Truth is cast not into a void, but to preservers, historical men. It comes from nothing, but is addressed to a people. Three factors are involved in a people. The first is the people's 'endowment', their 'earth': the land on which they live and which they cultivate, but also relatively permanent features of their world such as the German language that they speak. The second is the ordinary and traditional, the old 'world', their pagan customs and beliefs, for example. The third is the new 'world', their 'withheld vocation', the beginnings, say, of Christianity among them (OWA, 75 L). The creation of, say, a Christian work of art cannot be explained by these factors, especially not by the old world. But it is guided by them. It is composed in German, adapted to their endowment, and it presents a Christian message. It makes the people's destiny explicit, and grounds it on their native soil.

Thirdly, founding is 'beginning'. A beginning is in a way direct or immediate, but it may also require long preparation – like a jump or leap (*Sprung*) for which we need to prepare ourselves. A genuine beginning is not simple or primitive; it contains the end latent within itself; it is a leap forward (*Vorsprung*), that leaps over everything to come (OWA, 76). Homer's epics, for example, are not primitive or simple; they also implicitly contain the tragedies which later opened up the world of the Greek city-states. The history of art is not a steady cumulative process, but is punctuated by massive explosions of creative energy that leave future generations to do what they can with the pieces.

'When beings as a whole require grounding in openness, art always attains to its historical essence as founding' (OWA, 75). Such art alters our whole view of being. This has happened three times in the West. First, and most radically, in Greece, with its conception of being as 'presence' *(Anwesenheit)*. Then in medieval times, when the beings disclosed by the Greeks were transformed into things created, by God. And finally in modern times, when beings become 'objects', to be calculated and manipulated. (This is what lies at the root of 'technology'.) Each time a new world arises; unconcealment of beings happens; and it sets itself into work, a setting accomplished by art. When art happens, a thrust enters history and history begins again. Art grounds history, not history in the sense of important events, but history as the entry of a people into its native endowments and its movement towards its appointed destiny. Now we understand the word 'origin' in the title of the essay. 'Origin', *Ursprung*, means a 'leap forth' (OWA, 77 L). Art lets truth leap forth. Art is the origin or leaping forth of the work of art. Thus it is the origin of the creators and preservers of the work, and that means of the existence of a historical people.

The End of Art?

Like BT, this work ends with a discussion of Hegel (OWA, 79–81). Is art, Heidegger asks, still an essential and necessary way in which that truth happens which is decisive for our historical existence? Hegel answered that it is not. But Hegel's answer was given in the framework of a truth of beings that has already happened, the truth that has informed Western thought since the Greeks. If ever Hegel's claim comes up for decision, the decision will involve a quite different conception of truth.

At present we are too entangled in the old conception to assess Hegel's claim. All we can do is continue to reflect on art. This cannot force art into existence, but it prepares for it: 'Only such knowledge prepares a space for art, a way for creators, a location for preservers' (OWA, 78). Heidegger conceives himself as a sort of John the Baptist for the new art and the new world that is to come.

The Turn

Heidegger used the word 'turn' (*Kehre*) to refer to two things: the shift of perspective involved in the transition from Divisions I and II of BT, the analytic of Dasein, to Division III, on being and time; and the change from forgetfulness of being to the remembrance of it that he hoped would come. Often 'the turn' is used to refer to a change in Heidegger's own thought which supposedly occurred in about 1930. Can we detect signs of a turn in this third sense? Has Heidegger changed his mind between BT and OWA?

There is plainly much continuity between the two works. Heidegger is still concerned with Dasein and its world. But the focus of interest has changed. BT was concerned with the nature of Dasein in an already established world. OWA asks a different question: How is a world set up in the first place? Heidegger approaches this question through a series of increasingly fundamental works of art. First, a Van Gogh, which reveals to us a world that is already in place. Second, a temple, which is often the dominant, structuring centre of a city-state. Here he also refers to tragedies, which originated in a particular city-state, though they were often performed in other cities. And finally, though implicitly, the Panhellenic poetry of Homer and Hesiod, poetry regarded as the common possession of the Greek world.

Heidegger no doubt exaggerates. Is art always so crucial for world-building as it perhaps was for the Greeks? Was the Christian world set up by art or only celebrated (or set forth) by art? Might not equipment – the first motor-car or the Concorde plane – set up a world as effectively as an artwork? Is every dominant, world-structuring monument (such as Trafalgar Square) a great work of art? But these queries are by the way. The main point is that Dasein cannot play the pivotal part in the founding of a world. It cannot, as it does in the first two divisions of BT, occupy the centre of the stage.

From Dasein to Being

Dasein is essentially in the world. Ordinary human discoveries, communications, decisions, and activities presuppose a familiar background of values and categories, customs and routines. How does this world get established? How for that matter can it be radically changed? Not by ordinary Dasein, for Dasein is always already in a world. By extraordinary Dasein, then? The artist, the poet, or even the thinker? Heidegger, in the wake of Hölderlin, sometimes describes the poet as a sort of demigod, standing in a no man's land between the gods and the people, and transmitting the hints of the gods to the people. It is in this no man's land that it is decided who man is and where he establishes his existence (HEP).

The artist or the poet cannot do his work in any normal human way, in any way that already presupposes the world that he is to set up. He must be something like the vehicle of an impersonal force – art or truth or being itself. The artist must be 'resolute', *entschlossen*, ecstatically 'opened up' to this force. The resoluteness that originally seemed to be a way of conducting oneself authentically in this world has found a new role: resoluteness enables the creator, and the preservers, to found a new world.

Language too has found a new role. In BT language grows out of the significant involvements of the already established world. In OWA it plays a more fundamental part. Projective language, the naming of things for the first time, helps to found a world. Language too cannot be devised by human beings in the normal human way, which already presupposes our possession of language. So language too, at least projective language, is an impersonal force that constitutes Dasein and its world, not simply an instrument for communication. This is why Heidegger says: 'Language speaks, not man. Man only speaks when he fatefully answers to language' (PR, 96).

The Original Leap

Has Heidegger's thought changed? Or is it only his questions that have changed? Or have new questions simply developed out of his earlier questions? Perhaps we should attend to what he says about the 'beginning'. A genuine beginning, he said, is not simple or primitive, it leaps over what is to come. Might this be true of his own early work? OWA, for example, speaks of earth as the counterpart to world. BT, by contrast, makes no reference to 'earth'. Yet already in lectures of 1925 Heidegger spoke of 'earth' as that on which the world of our work and activity rests (xx. 269–70). Earth is not yet, as in OWA, in conflict with world. It is a familiar outlying part of our world, the semi-domesticated nature on which we graze our cows. It is not, as in OWA, the threatening, hostile, if indispensable, earth from which a world has to be wrested. But this is because the questions asked in the two works are different. The concept of earth remains inconspicuous in Heidegger's early works, but ready for a more significant role later on. The early Heidegger is perhaps the Homeric epic from which develop the tragedies and temples of the later Heidegger.

Chapter 11
St Martin of Messkirch?

Heidegger is above all a philosopher. The politics is peripheral. But we cannot forget that dark episode in the early 1930s, his entanglement with Nazism. What does it tell us about his philosophy? And conversely what does his philosophy tell us about it? Not much.

The Rector

In 1948 Heidegger wrote to an old pupil, Herbert Marcuse, that in 1933 he 'expected from National Socialism a spiritual renewal of life in its entirety, a reconciliation of social antagonisms and a deliverance of Western Dasein from the dangers of communism' (Wolin, 162). Some of his supporters justify his decision on the ground that Nazism was at that time the only alternative to communism. Why prefer Nazism to communism? The modern world, as BT portrays it, is out of joint. But there is little in BT to favour Nazism rather than communism or, say, a resolute withdrawal from public life. Heidegger was a conservative, preferring variety and rank to 'levelling', the uniformity and egalitarianism that he associated with the USA and the Soviet Union. He was, even after his disenchantment with Nazism, intensely patriotic, believing that the fate of the West would be decided in Germany, though by German philosophy rather than by German arms. But other conservatives and patriots, such as Spengler and Jünger, resisted the allure of Nazism. Is not Nazism intrinsically evil? One can say: 'I am a

communist, but I do not support show trials or forced collectivization.'
But one can hardly say: 'I am a Nazi, but I do not favour anti-Semitism
or the Holocaust.' The vices of communism are incidental to it, while
those of Nazism seem to be of its essence.

However, much of what is now in the past was, in 1933, still in the
future. Hitler had in 1924 been briefly imprisoned for an attempted
coup in Bavaria. But he learned from his mistakes and had now come
to power by legal means. Hitler was, it is true, anti-Semitic. But anti-
Semitism had not yet acquired the taboo that it has now, when it
automatically disqualifies a politician or movement from consideration.
No one at that time (except Hitler himself) dreamed of exterminating
Jews. Nazism offered many attractions besides anti-Semitism: a new
deal for the unemployed, relief from the ravages of technology and
capitalism, the repudiation of the Versailles Treaty, a return to
traditional ('family') values, a cult of youth. Words that *in German* now
serve as alarm-signals – *Führer*, *Volk*, *entschlossen* – sounded in 1933 as
innocent as their English counterparts still do: the strong 'leader', with
his 'leadership qualities', and the 'people' or 'nation' in need of
'decisive' leadership. (A *Volk* is not a 'race'. Biological racism is alien to
Heidegger's philosophy.) Nazism did not then have the solidified
essence that it now has. Who knows, asked Heidegger in 1945, 'what
would have happened and what could have been averted if in 1933 all
available powers had arisen . . . to purify and moderate the movement
that had come to power?' (Wolin, 16). He thought that he could
influence the future course of Nazism. This seems absurd now that
Nazism has unfolded its 'true' nature. But it did not seem so in 1933.
Heidegger saw Nazism in terms of its possibilities, not its sheer
actuality.

If the ideas of BT did not commit Heidegger to Nazism, might they not
have immunized him against it? It is asking too much of a philosophy
to expect it to secure us against a skilled political manipulator who
learns from his mistakes, a masterly tactician with an impeccable sense

10. Heidegger's grave in the Messkirch cemetery

of timing. No ethic, no list of rights and wrongs, will do the trick either. No file of past villains, of anti-heroes, will work. The accomplished villain knows how to keep himself out of the file and look like a hero. Nor is it only villains we must be on guard against: people often get into a mess without the help of conspicuous villains. (The search for villains to blame for the mess is often a part of the mess.) Against all this, philosophy can provide no unfailing amulet. As Heidegger tells us, we live towards a future that is as yet unknown to us, with no incontestable guidance from the past.

The Thinker

Where does Heidegger stand as a philosopher? Many of his central ideas owe something to his contemporaries and predecessors. The turn from epistemology to ontology was taken before Heidegger by Nicolai Hartmann. The idea of Dasein is developed in critical engagement with Husserl's phenomenology and with Max Scheler's philosophical anthropology. The notions of *Existenz*, *Angst*, and *Augenblick* stem from Kierkegaard and, more immediately, from Jaspers. Heidegger himself acknowledges the influence of Dilthey, and more especially Dilthey's friend Yorck von Wartenburg, on his own view of history (BT, 397–404). He is less eager to admit the influence of Spengler, who had imputed to the Greeks the notion of being as presence and stressed the role of destiny in history.

Is Heidegger's thought just a *bricolage* of ideas derived from others? No. Heidegger's thought reaches back far beyond his contemporaries and immediate predecessors, back as far as the ancient Greeks. This insulates him against the direct influence of his contemporaries, or, indeed, of any single philosopher or school. For example, he traces the concept of Angst not simply back to Kierkegaard, but to Luther and St Augustine. He claims, in fact, that he developed his view of Dasein as care in trying to square the 'Augustinian (i.e. Helleno–Christian) anthropology' with the 'ontology of Aristotle' (BT, 199 n. vii).

Heidegger clearly does not adopt the ideas and problems current in his immediate environment without more ado. At the very least he unearths their remoter ancestry. And almost invariably he confers on his borrowings his own characteristic stamp, integrating them into a context in which their alien origins are scarcely visible. Not only this. As often as not Heidegger repays his debts by reinterpreting the philosopher who made the loan. How much does Heidegger owe to Kant? Or to Aristotle? It is not easy to say, because Heidegger interprets Kant and Aristotle in terms of his own thought. Seen through Heidegger's eyes Kant and Aristotle are as much in Heidegger's debt as he is in theirs. His readings of other philosophers are usually not easy to accept. But equally they are not easy to forget, and once we have encountered Heidegger's interpretation of a philosopher it is hard to read him through wholly non-Heideggerian eyes.

If the influence of others on Heidegger is a tricky matter, so too is his influence on others. On the face of it his influence is immense: on theologians (Bultmann, Rahner, Tillich), on psychoanalysts (Ludwig Binswanger), on literary critics (Emil Staiger), as well as on philosophers (Sartre, Merleau-Ponty, Levinas, Ortega y Gasset, Gadamer, and Derrida). But how long will his influence last? Will Heidegger live as long as Aristotle or even Kant? It is not easy to say. It will depend on events that we cannot foresee, on what others, philosophers and non-philosophers, do in the future, on what they do with Heidegger and what they do without him.

The question of Heidegger's influence depends too on the answer to a different question: What is Heidegger's stature as a thinker? This too is difficult to answer. Heidegger did not simply give solutions to problems that exercised other philosophers, so that we can measure his stature by comparing his solutions with those given by others. He asks new questions, questions that he perhaps cannot answer, but which he believes to be more fundamental than the general run of

133

questions. How are we to assess the significance of his questions, or indeed of such answers as he gave to them? Again this will depend, in part at least, on what others do about Heidegger in the future. The question of Heidegger's merit is not sharply distinct from the question of his influence.

The Man

Heidegger is now, though not wholly perspicuous, less enigmatic than he was at the beginning. He was ambitious for status and influence. He was a relentless thinker, who tried to redraw the map of philosophy. He was a restless, tormented man, tormented not only by philosophy but also by his ambiguous Christian faith. In these respects he resembles no one so much as St Augustine.

Further Reading

The best account of Heidegger's life available in English is *Martin Heidegger: A Political Life*, by H. Ott (London, 1993). Heidegger's lifelong friend H. W. Petzet gives an interesting and sympathetic portrait of him in *Encounters and Dialogues with Martin Heidegger, 1929–1976* (Chicago, 1993).

A good starting-point for a study of Heidegger's own works is his *Basic Writings*, ed. D. F. Krell (London, 2nd edn, 1993). This contains the introduction to BT, OWA, and nine other essays. Some of Heidegger's lectures are easier going than BT itself and make a good introduction to it. The translations of xx, xxiv, and xxvi are especially recommended. The lectures on Nietzsche, ed. D. F. Krell (New York, 1979–87) provide an attractive and accessible introduction to Heidegger's later thought.

There are several good commentaries on BT. *Heidegger on Being Human*, by R. Schmitt (New York, 1969), stresses the similarity between Heidegger and Wittgenstein. H. L. Dreyfus, in *Being-in-the-World: A Commentary on Heidegger's Being and Time, Division I* (Cambridge, Mass., 1991), pits Heidegger against the 'artificial intelligence' model of the human mind. J. Richardson's *Existential Epistemology: A Heideggerian Critique of the Cartesian Project* (Oxford, 1986) can profitably be read alongside L. Stevenson, 'Heidegger on Cartesian Scepticism', *British Journal for the History of Philosophy*, 1/1 (Feb. 1993), 81–98. Also useful are

M. Gelven, *A Commentary on Heidegger's 'Being and Time'* (New York, 1970) and S. Mulhall, *Heidegger and Being and Time* (London, 1996).

For a brief overall account of Heidegger's thought, O. Pöggeler, *Martin Heidegger's Path of Thinking* (Atlantic Highlands, NJ, 1987) can be recommended. *Heidegger: A Critical Reader*, ed. H. L. Dreyfus and H. Hall (Oxford, 1992), and *The Cambridge Companion to Heidegger*, ed. C. Guignon (Cambridge, 1993), contain essays covering the full range of his thought. G. Steiner's *Heidegger* (London, 2nd edn, 1992) also deals with his thought as a whole.

Two recent monographs tackle the whole of Heidegger's thought in a lucid and engaging fashion. H. Philipse, *Heidegger's Philosophy of Being: A Critical Interpretation* (Princeton University Press, 1998) is a long and thorough treatment. R. Polt, *Heidegger: An Introduction* (University of London Press, 1999) covers the same ground more briefly. For useful guidance through the complexities of Heidegger's vocabulary, *A Heidegger Dictionary* by M. Inwood (Blackwell: Oxford, 1999) should be consulted.

Glossary

ableben; Ableben to die or decease as a living organism; demise, biological death

Anwesenheit presence (e.g. of someone at a place or event). Cf. the Greek *parousia*, 'presence' (from *ousia*, 'being, substance')

Augenblick moment, moment of vision

auslegen; Auslegung to spread or lay out, to interpret; interpretation

Befindlichkeit state of mind, how one finds oneself, how one is doing, from *(sich) befinden*, 'to find (oneself)', etc. (as in *Wie befinden sie sich?* (1) 'How do you do?' (2) 'How do you feel?') and *befindlich*, 'to be found' in a place

besorgen; Besorgen to provide, make provision; concern. It applies to one's dealings with tools and equipment

bewusst, Bewusstsein conscious; consciousness (of objects), conscious being, being conscious. Heidegger avoids these words, which were favourites of Hegel and Husserl. But his use of *Dasein* is modelled on *Bewusstsein*, which is also used both concretely and abstractly

da; das Da there, here; the There

damals then (in the past), on that former occasion

dann then (in the future)

dasein; Dasein to be there (in non-Heideggerian German: to exist); *Dasein*, being-there, human being, being human. Heidegger uses *Dasein* to refer *both* to the (concrete) human being *and* to its (abstract) being human. In BT *Dasein* usually refers to an entity, the human being. In lectures Heidegger often speaks of 'human [*menschliche*] Dasein' and 'the Dasein of man'

destruieren; Destruktion to destroy; destruction. But Heidegger uses these words in a sense close to 'deconstruct(ion)' and perhaps to Hegel's *aufheben, Aufhebung*, meaning 'kick(ing) upstairs', at once 'cancelling, preserving, and elevating'

dichten; Dichtung, dichterisch to compose, devise, invent, feign; composition, fiction, invention, poem, poetry; poetic, inventive

eigentlich; Eigentlichkeit authentic, real; authenticity. This is related to the adjective *eigen*, 'own', 'personal'. To be authentic is to be true to one's 'own self', to be one's own person, to do one's own thing

Ekstase; ekstatisch ecstasis; ecstatic. Literally 'standing forth'

entschliessen; entschlossen; Entschlossenheit to resolve; resolute; resoluteness. From *schliessen*, 'to close'; hence literally 'to disclose', etc.

erschliessen; Erschlossenheit to disclose; disclosedness

existieren; Existenz; existenzial, existenziell; Existenzial lit. to stand forth, to exist; standing forth, existence; existential (adjective); *existentiell*; existential (noun). The adjectives *existenzial* and *existenziell* differ in the same way as *ontologisch* and *ontisch*, except that they apply only to Dasein. To choose to be a soldier rather than a cobbler is to make an *existentiell* choice. The capacity to make such choices, and the philosopher's understanding of it, are existential

faktisch; Faktizität factical, facticity; similar to 'factual, factuality' except that they are applied only to Dasein, e.g. the sheer fact that one exists

Fürsorge solicitude, one's attitude to other human beings

Gegenwart; gegenwärtig; gegenwärtigen the present, lit. waiting towards; (in the) present; to make present

Geist; geistig spirit, mind; spiritual, intellectual. These occur rarely in BT

Gerede idle talk, chatter

geschehen to happen, historize

Geschichte; geschichtlich; geschichtlichkeit history; historical;

historicality. In Heidegger's usage, these words concern history as happening or events, not the study of events (*Historie*). *Geschichte* also means 'story, narrative', and this may influence Heidegger's use of it

Geschick destiny (of a group or community)

gewesen; Gewesenheit having been (past tense of *sein*); having-beenness, the (living) past

Gewissen conscience. *Gewissen* is related to *gewiss*, 'certain', but BT, 291 dissociates conscience from certainty

Historie; historisch history, historiography, historiology; historical, historiographical, historiological

Horizont horizon. But as Heidegger uses it, it means the realm bounded by a horizon or the vantage point from which we can survey such a realm

jetzt; das Jetzt now; the now, instant

kehren; die Kehre to turn; the turn(ing), esp. (1) from forgetfulness of being to remembrance of it; (2) from Divisions I and II of BT to Division III; (3) from the early to the late Heidegger

Licht; lichten; Lichtung light, brightness; to clear (e.g. a forest); clearing (of a forest, but, in Heidegger, of openness, the There, etc.), a clearing (in a forest), open space. For Heidegger, *Lichtung* retains its link with light and lighting

man; das Man one, they, etc.; the 'they'

Neugier curiosity, thirst for novelty

ontisch; ontologisch; Ontologie ontical; ontological; ontology. Proper ontology deals not with beings (*das Seiende*), but with being (*das Sein*), either the being of some specific 'region' of beings or, if it is 'fundamental ontology', being as such. A claim, enquiry, etc. is ontological if it concerns the *being* of entities, if, roughly, it is *a priori*. It is ontical if it concerns only beings or entities, if, roughly, it is empirical

Poesie poetry, poem = *Dichtung* in a narrow sense

reden; Rede to talk; talk, discourse

reissen; Riss; Grundriss to seize, snatch, tear; tearing, (a) tear, fissure, rift, draft, drawing, sketch, design; ground-plan, sketch, outline, paradigm

Schicksal fate (of an individual)

sein; das Seiende; das Sein to be; the being, the entity, what is, beings, entities; being, Being. The distinction between *das Seiende* and *das Sein* is crucial for Heidegger. In xxiv and thereafter he called it the 'ontological difference' (*ontologische Differenz*)

sorgen; Sorge to worry, take care of, provide for, see to; care, worry, trouble, careful attention

springen; Sprung; Vorsprung to leap, jump, spring; (a) leap, jump, spring; (a) leap, etc. before, forwards (also a 'projection', and a 'start' or 'advantage')

sterben; das Sterben to die; dying

stiften; Stiftung to found, create, establish, endow; foundation, establishment, endowment, bequest. Hence, for Heidegger, 'founding', with the senses of (1) 'bestowing'; (2) 'grounding'; (3) 'beginning'

stimmen; Stimmung to harmonize, to tune, to put someone into a certain mood; tuning, mood, temper, disposition

Tod; Sein zum Tode; Freiheit zum Tode death; being towards death; freedom towards death

Ursprung, ursprünglich; gleichursprünglich source, origin, lit. leap forth; original, primordial; equiprimordial, equally original

verfallen; das Verfallen to fall, deteriorate; falling, deterioration

Vergehen; Vergangen; tfie Vergangenheit to pass (away), elapse, disappear; past, gone by, bygone; the (dead) past

Volk people, nation. This is an ethnic or cultural concept rather than a biological concept, as 'race' (*Rasse*) is; to be a member of the German *Volk* is to speak German, to follow German customs, and to think of oneself as German

Vorhabe, Vorsicht, Vorgriff fore-having; fore-sight; fore-conception. This 'fore-structure' (*Vor-struktur*) is involved in all interpretation (BT, 327)

vorhanden available, extant, present at hand. In contrast to *zuhanden*, it applies to what is (or is seen as) simply there, neutral, colourless, disengaged from human activities and purposes

Welt; Umwelt; Lebenswelt, in der Welt, innerweltlich; weltlich; Weltlichkeit world; environment, world around (one, us); life-world; in the world (only of Dasein); within the world (only of things other than Dasein); worldly (of the world); worldhood (of the world). Heidegger distinguishes four senses of *Welt*: (1) the aggregate of all present-at-hand entities; (2) the being of such entities, or a particular 'region' of them (e.g. numbers etc. are 'the world of the mathematician'); (3) the world in which Dasein lives, either the '"public" we-world, or one's "own" closest (domestic) *Umwelt*'; (4) worldhood, the basic structure of a world. He generally uses *Welt* in sense 3 (BT, 64f.)

werfen; geworfen; Geworfenheit throw; thrown; thrownness. Cf. *entwerfen; Entwurf*: to throw off, away, to sketch, design; sketch, design, project

Werk work. In OWA Heidegger uses phrases that mean *both* 'put to work, set going' *and* 'put into the work (of art)'

Zeit; zeitlich, Zeitlichkeit; innerzeitig, zeitigen time; temporal (only of Dasein); temporality (only of Dasein); within time (only of what is other than Dasein); to ripen, mature, temporalize (of temporality)

zuhanden ready to hand, handy, available for human use. It applies esp. to *Zeug*, tool(s), equipment, gear

Zukunft; zukünftig the future (as coming towards); future, futural

zweideutig; Zweideutigkeit ambiguous, double-dealing; ambiguity, duplicity

Index

Note: Martin Heidegger is referred to as 'MH' in sub-entries

Expand your collection of
VERY SHORT INTRODUCTIONS